adoption
piece by piece

SPECIAL NEEDS

Edited by Sara Graefe

D0122045

Published by
Groundwork Press
101-2780 Broadway
Vancouver, BC V5M 1Y8

Cover and book design by Elyssa Schmid, Radiant Design
Additional design by Jennifer Lee and Lissa Cowan

Printed in Canada by Hignell Book Printing

National Library of Canada Cataloguing in Publication Data

Main entry under title:
Special needs/edited by Sara Graefe

(Adoption piece by piece)
Includes bibliographic references and index.

ISBN 0-914539-23-X

1. Adoptive parents—Canada. 2. Special needs adoption—
Canada. I. Graefe, Sara. II. Series
HV888.S63 2003   362.73′4′0870971   C2003-911026-5

This series is dedicated to special needs
adoptive families everywhere

table of contents

MENTAL HEALTH

INSTITUTIONS AND CHILDREN

TRANSITION TO ADULTHOOD FOR PEOPLE WITH SPECIAL NEEDS

foreword

This book, and the trilogy it is part of, began creative life as a concept for a booklet about adoption of children who have special needs. It was soon apparent however that there were far more issues, ideas and excellent, relevant material to be contained in a small booklet and the project scope grew to a book and when that grew too massive, finally to the current trilogy.

Each of the three books in this series stands on its own as a complete work on a particular area of adoption interest but it is all three books together that cover the spectrum of special needs adoption issues.

A project of this scope requires the effort of a great number of people to come to fruition. There is space here to mention only some of those involved. To everyone else who contributed to this project I can only express my regret at not acknowledging you directly, though you know who you are and that your contribution is greatly appreciated.

First, I must offer my thanks to all the individual article authors who have given so generously of their thoughts and work. Special thanks must go to Sara Graefe, the chief author/editor on this project. It was under her skilled and steady hand that this series actually took shape. Those thanks must also extend to our editorial and design team of Lissa Cowan, Jennifer Lee and, from Radiant Design, Elyssa Schmidt who diligently kept the work moving and gave form and life to the final product.

I want to thank the Ministry for Children and Families for their support for this project. And I especially want to thank Susan Lees of the Queen Alexandra Centre for Children's Health, Adoption Support program for her support, and the Queen Alexandra Foundation for their generous grant to support the publication of these books.

In the end though, this series was inspired by the dedication, commitment, wisdom, exhaustion and love of the families who have embarked on the lifelong special needs adoption journey. The road they are on is not an easy one, but their journey is filled with hope and possibility.

It is to the families that this series is dedicated.

Brad Watson
Executive Director
May, 2003

introduction

Who We Are

In 1987, a group of ten overwhelmed parents in British Columbia came together to share experiences after adopting children with special needs. Burnt out (and often feeling burned) by systems and other organizations that didn't understand, these folks needed the reassurance and support from others *living it* that they weren't crazy or bad parents – that the challenges they were facing with their children simply came with the terrain of special needs adoption. The sense of comfort, support and community generated by these meetings was profound – so much so that these parents began advocating for similar services for other special needs adoptive families in BC. Through their efforts, the Society of Special Needs Adoptive Parents (SNAP) came into being. SNAP became a non-profit society and charity in 1988, and received its first grant from the provincial government in 1989. It was a small sum of money, but just enough to open an office and hire a few staff to get the message out that something was available addressing the very special struggles of special needs adoptive families. Call it the law of the jungle, but once that message got out, word spread like wild fire – demand for SNAP's services literally exploded and has never slowed down.

What started around a kitchen table has grown into a province-wide information, education and support service for parents, professionals, and others touched by special needs and adoption issues. SNAP has established an extensive peer support network throughout BC, with trained Resource Parents and over a dozen peer support groups, providing one-to-one and mutual support to fellow special needs adoptive parents. Through the support network, an extensive library, web site, and bi-monthly newsmagazine, along with the efforts of volunteers and an ever-growing staff, SNAP continues to ensure that the organization is accessible to all special needs adoptive families throughout the province. The Society has also established a reputation as a leading adoption resource in Canada. Over the years, we have received information requests from as far afield as Hawaii, the United Kingdom, Africa, Australia, and New Zealand.

About the Series *Adoption Piece by Piece*

Parenting any child can be challenging, even at the best of times. Parenting an adopted child with special needs presents a unique set of psychological, emotional and financial challenges. This three-volume series book speaks to the many issues faced by the special needs adoptive families and professionals in the field who access our services. Volume one explores core, lifelong issues in adoption, as well as cross-cultural and diversity issues. Volume two focuses on prevalent special needs issues that affect today's adopted children. Volume three is a toolkit for adoptive parents, providing a range of support and advocacy tips, as well as specific sections on how to advocate and work within various societal systems.

The series covers a wide terrain and strives, like SNAP's services, to provide information, education and support. The factual articles – which aim to arm you with the information you need – are interspersed with more personal perspectives from adoptive parents who are living with the issue in question, with the hope that these individual voices will help support and inspire those of you struggling with similar issues. Where possible we've tried to include pieces with a local or Canadian context. Many of the articles have been pulled from the archives of the ever-popular SNAP newsletter-turned-newsmagazine. We're also grateful to have received permission to reprint a number of articles from top American adoption specialists and publications. The result is a veritable grab bag of information, covering the whole gamut of adoption and special needs parenting issues.

What is Special Needs Adoption?

For those of you who might be new to special needs adoption, let's start by clarifying a few terms. When the public-at-large hears the word "adoption," most people think they know what it entails. In fact, they often don't – at least not in its full implications and complexities. "Adoption" typically conjures images of family, pretty much like any other family, except that the kid might not look much like Mom or Dad. We may think of loving parents who open their hearts and their homes to little ones without a permanent family – or about kids who bring the joys and laughter of childhood into the lives of couples who struggle with infertility.

Yes, adoption can certainly be these things. And of course, parents hope for the very best when they choose to build a family through adoption. But adoption is also about a whole spectrum of issues, some of which aren't always comfortable – including grief and loss, attachment issues, and identity issues to name a few. Adoption today is very different than it was 50, 60 years ago. Gone are the days from the 1950s when there were more healthy infants in need of homes than prospective adoptive families. Nowadays, the adoption of children with special needs – kids who were once considered "hard to place" or "unadoptable" – has become the norm rather than the exception. These include children with physical or mental disabilities, children with a history of abuse and neglect, sibling groups placed together, older children, and children adopted internationally.

Adopted children with special needs are extremely complex individuals who often are living with conditions and have survived traumas that are far beyond your own realm of experience. Parenting these children can be a complicated, demanding, stressful undertaking that pushes you to limits you didn't even know you had. Sometimes love isn't enough to help these children deal with past wounds or debilitating medical conditions. Special parenting strategies, interventions, and professional services and supports are often necessary.

That said, special needs adoption can also be a unique, rewarding experience. Many families have found it fulfilling for a whole host of reasons – from gaining a renewed sense of hope in the world by giving a child a home and standing by that child on their life journey, to growing stronger as a family by working together to meet new challenges. Even some of the parents who've weathered the worst pitfalls with their special needs adoptive children are still able to speak of the positives and the life-affirming experiences they've gained.

What Do We Mean by Post-Adoption Support, Anyway?

At SNAP, we recognize that adoption is a life-long process – it's not something that's over once you sign the completion papers, or the judge grants the adoption order. When you decide to bring a child into your home through adoption, you're making a lifetime commitment to that child. In many cases, you are giving a child with special needs the chance to grow up in a permanent family – to have someone there at their side as they walk through life, to hold their hand when they need support, and to have a place to call home.

Our work with families over the years has proven to us (and this has been supported by adoption research) that access to appropriate, adoption-sensitive supports throughout the lifecycle is not only desirable but *crucial*, both to meet the child's special needs and to build healthy adoptive families. And this book has been designed to reflect this philosophy. "Post-adoption support" isn't just about what to do when you first get your child home; it's about having supports in place for the rest of your lives. We've presented a wealth of information on a variety of topics that you may encounter at one point or another during your life journey with your adopted child.

Face it: our children are special. As we mentioned earlier, many of these kids were once considered "hard to place" or "unadoptable", and would have spent their childhoods in institutions. Even today, many of Canada's "waiting children" spend considerable time in high-end foster homes prior to adoption, with experienced caregivers and access to funded, specialized services to deal with their extraordinary special needs. Giving a child a permanent home doesn't take away their care requirements. Parenting these kids can be especially challenging, and you deserve all the support you can get to meet your child's needs, and to help give that child their best shot at life.

How to Use This Series of Books

There is no such thing as a "how-to" parenting manual – just as there's no single, "right" way to parent an adopted child with special needs. Each child is unique, and as a parent you are likely your own best expert on your child. These three books are here to guide you and to provide signposts along the way, as you face uncertainty or new situations, navigate troubled waters, or simply need affirmation that you're on the right path.

Each book in the series has been designed as a resource, yet another pillar in your multi-faceted support structure. (And if you're thinking, "support structure, what support structure?!", don't worry – we give you tips and ideas throughout on how to build one, or how to maintain and strengthen the one you already have in place.)

Don't let the size of the collection overwhelm you. Our intent was to cover a whole range of issues that may be encountered by special needs adoptive families. We don't expect you to sit down and read each volume from cover to cover in chronological order ("and there will be a test tomorrow") – although you can certainly do that if you like. Think instead of a grab bag, and dip in as needed, depending on what issues you are currently facing with your child. You might find it most useful to start with the chapters or sections that apply most to your own situation. That said, there may also be helpful information and strategies in other chapters that can be adapted to fit your circumstances. Remember, too, that your experiences and concerns may shift and change over time, as your child grows and changes. You may find yourself returning to certain chapters over and over again, sometimes reading the same old material with a new perspective.

The material covered in these books is just the beginning. At the end of each volume, we've included detailed resource lists, pointing you towards other books, videos, web sites, and organizations dealing with the issues covered in that section. We hope that you make use of these lists to continue to educate yourself, advocate for your child, and build a solid support structure for your family.

Keeping Afloat in Times of Change

As this book goes to press, the social services system in British Columbia is undergoing intense change. Balancing the budget while reducing taxes is the government's bottom line, and we've already seen the beginnings of massive restructuring, huge service cuts, and new user fees for services in our sector. It is hard predict what things will look like in the next six months, let alone the next six years. Naturally, this is causing a lot of anxiety for special needs adoptive parents, many of whom rely on government services, or the support of provincially funded agencies such as SNAP.

At SNAP, meanwhile, we're rapidly approaching fifteen years of service to special needs adoptive parents in BC and beyond. And we hope to be here for another 15 years – 30 years, 45 years, or as long as families continue to adopt special needs children. But the reality is, our future is uncertain. Now more than ever, adoptive parents need the tools to advocate for services and supports for their children and families, and to find creative ways to continue to build supports for themselves at a grassroots level. This book, in a sense, is our legacy to you, regardless of what happens to SNAP as we currently know it. It is our sincere hope that you will use this book as a continued source of support well into the future.

A Final Word

We'd like to thank the British Columbia Ministry for Children and Families Development, and the Adoption Support Program at the Queen Alexandra Centre for Children's Health in Victoria, for providing generous funding to assist with the creation and publication of this volume.

And we'd like to dedicate the book to the people we serve – special needs adoptive parents, and all those touched by adoption and special needs issues. We hope that this resource will help you better understand, support and appreciate your very special child.

Sara Graefe, Editor
Society of Special Needs Adoptive Parents
Vancouver, 2003

special needs

The majority of adoptions today are considered "special needs." This is a big change from the 50s and 60s when there were more healthy infants in Canada in need of homes than prospective adoptive families. Today's waiting children are typically children with physical or mental disabilities, children with a history of abuse and neglect, sibling groups, and older children. People sometimes mistakenly believe that special needs are only an issue in domestic adoption. However, special needs issues are just as prevalent in international adoption. After all, adoption is about kids with baggage. All children arrive in their adoptive families with a past, whether they're from down the street or the other side of the world.

This is the second book in a three-part series for adoptive parents. In this volume, we focus on a number of special needs conditions that are prevalent in adoption today. "Special needs" can mean a variety of things. The term most commonly refers to a special condition or disability affecting the child, be it medical (e.g. FAS, malnutrition, etc.), physical (e.g. cerebral palsy, spina bifida, etc.), emotional and behavioural (e.g. attachment disorder, conduct disorder, etc.), or historical (e.g., history of abuse and neglect; multiple foster home placements; institutionalisation overseas; etc.). "Special needs" can also refer to special placement needs – children who are adopted over the age of two, sibling groups who are placed in the same home either concurrently or consecutively, culturally compatible placements (such as aboriginal placements), and foster-to-adopt situations.

Prevalent Special Needs Conditions
There is a wide range of conditions you might encounter with your child, from Fragile X Syndrome to FAS to encephylolyptomanosis. Obviously, it is impossible for us to address them all in one volume. However, we touch on some of the most prevalent special needs conditions you'll encounter in the adoption community, including **invisible** and learning disabilities, **Fetal Alcohol Syndrome (FAS), Neonatal Abstinence Syndrome (NAS)/Pre-natal drug exposure, Attention Deficit Disorder** with and without hyperactivity **(ADD/ADHD), Conduct Disorder**, history of **abuse and neglect**, and **post-institutionalisation**. We launch

the volume by looking at **normal vs. "abnormal" development** to place our discussion of special needs in context, and we finish by addressing concerns around the **transition to adulthood** for your child with special needs.

Adoption as a Special Need

Some argue that all adopted people have "special needs" by virtue of being adopted – "special needs" in terms of attachment and identity issues, for example. We cover these adoption-specific issues in depth in the first volume of this series, *Lifelong Issues*. Please note that information on Attachment Disorder and special placement needs (i.e. cross-cultural adoption and sibling placements) is also to be found in this first volume.

Other Special Needs Conditions

A special note to parents whose child has *other* special needs not on this list: if the condition you're facing isn't named or discussed here, it doesn't mean that it's less important, or that it doesn't have a significant impact on your family. It may simply be less common. We encourage you to find all the information you can about your child's particular special needs. Educate yourself, the professionals in your child's life, and the public at large. The SNAP library is a great place to start. If we don't have what you're looking for, we'll do what we can to help you find it.

Further Reading

If you've found this volume helpful, please consider reading the other two books in this series: *Lifelong Issues* and *A Toolkit for Parents*.

For tips on how to use this book, please see the Introduction to the Series *Adoption Piece by Piece* on page 11.

A Brief Look at Normal & Abnormal Behaviour & Growth

by Dr. Frank Kunstal

Infants (0-18 months)

During the first 9 months, the primary developmental needs of the child are for safety and protection, security, meeting of dependency needs, and trust in others. This period forms the earliest foundation for all human relating, and sets the stage for 'learning to learn.' During the 9-18 month period, children are gradually developing a more social, relationship centered, and independent way. They are gradually becoming psychologically separate from a parent and beginning to develop a sense of self. When they gain increased mobility, they are increasingly able to explore, and though intoxicated with their new found mobility, are also anxious and apprehensive about being physically separate from the mother. Children of this stage need a stable, available, nurturing carer, one who provides encouragement and assurance, with mother or father a "safe haven" from which they can venture out, and safely return.

Normal, Expectable Behavior

Early: 0-6 months

- Gradually alert to the world.
- Infant has capacity to be comforted.
- Has preferred figures, especially mother.
- Child gradually gains a full range of emotions.
- Crying to stimulate carer to make contact.
- Infants orients to and follows mother.
- Can play alone and busy self contentedly.
- Smiling, eye contact, vocalization, responding to caregiver.

Late: 6-9 months

- Developing stranger anxiety.

- Approaches, greets, pursues, and follows mother.
- Exhibits anxiety, physical discomfort, upset, or emotional withdrawal if parent leaves or is unavailable.
- Likes routines.
- Checking behavior increases when around unfamiliar others.
- Protests the absence of a caregiver.

Normal Abnormalities and Developmental "Quirks"
- Infant's emotional responses fluctuate widely, and some have difficulty becoming regulated and calm.
- Avoidance of contact after separation.
- Difficulty settling into a pattern.
- Difficulty being comforted, general fussiness.
- "Intoxication" with newly mastered molbility.

If Things Go Wrong
Unfulfilled early needs lead to inability to satisfy self or other needs later, lack of empathy, serious trust issues, learning problems, emotional emptiness, feelings of being entitled, self-absorption.
- Apathy.
- A failure to thrive.
- Sleeping and eating problems.
- Treating strangers similarly to mother.
- Social unresponsiveness.
- Failure to reciprocate relationships.
- Disinterest in the environment.

Toddlers (1.5 to 3 years)
In toddlerhood, clinging and physical proximity is replaced by vacillating between exploration away from the mother and periodic visual, verbal and physical reconnection to her—torn between independence and the regression to the dependency of a baby. At times, the child seems intoxicated with pleasure of new-found freedom. A mother's response to the child during this period is critical, staying emotionally available despite the toddler's comings and goings, there for refueling. The child at this age has development of social emotions, and learns to use language, and not just behavior, to communicate.

Normal, Expectable Behaviour
- Increasingly social.

- Checking behavior, exploration and increased curiosity.
- Expanding interest in the father.
- "Emotional refueling" with mother.
- Beginning sense of humor.
- Mimicking, modeling, and "impersonator" behavior.
- Will seek a care giver when hurt, frustrated, or tired.
- Increased language development allows the child more self-control and delay of gratification.
- Attention-seeking and craving.
- Excitement at accomplishments, intoxication with newfound mobility.
- Assertive, self-directed, defiant, and easily frustrated. At times, an "emotional roller coaster."
- Not yet recognizing others as truly different from self.
- Gradually able to self-soothe and comfort.

Normal Abnormalities and Developmental 'Quirks'
- May be indiscriminate in giving affection.
- Scattered play.
- Difficulty delaying gratification.
- At times, behavior is greatly vacillating.
- May appear emotionally or behaviorally out-of-control at times, particularly at separations.
- Language development might be scanty.

If Things Go Wrong
Disruption in development of sense of self, in gaining autonomy, language problems, control of aggression and negative emotions, problems relating to others, identity issues. Lots of these children are felt victims, place selves in positions to be used or hurt. Very hard for them to repress negative experiences and feelings about themselves, and thus, to control anger and negative emotion toward and about others.

- Lack of interest in exploration, sparse curiosity.
- Failure to develop the give-and-take of relating.
- Absence of stranger anxiety, will treat strangers similarly to mother.
- Inability to be soothed, comforted, or nurtured.
- Clinging, fearful behavior.
- Lack of interest in others.
- Avoidance of contact after separation from a caregiver, with obvious anger.

- Difficulty in modulating emotion.

Preschoolers (3 - 5 years old)
The child in the preschool age now has some sense of individuality. During this time the child becomes able to recall the essential goodness of mother...even when angry or frustrated with her or when she is away. During this stage the child develops magical and egocentric thinking, believing themselves to be the 'center' of all that occurs, feeling responsible or to blame for experiences to self or others. Due to the onset of the child's capacity for fantasy, imagination, and magical thinking, parents must help the child to separate the real from the fantasied, the imagined from the experienced. Children need to be encouraged, exposed to, and supported to have opportunities to use their new-found imagination/creativity/ and fantasy. Children of this stage need guidance, education, and interpretation of real or imagined experiences, fantasies. Some parents can too easily get caught in the dilemma of constant correction, education, or imposition of 'reality,' to the extent that the child's use of a critical developmental tool (fantasy and imagination) is thwarted. Also, as the child has an enhanced tendency toward self-blame (due to egocentric thinking), parent must avoid the use of guilt, harsh discipline, or comparisons to others as ways of controlling behavior.

Normal, Expectable Behavior
- Regresses when fatigued.
- Wants things his/her way.
- May show jealousy for one parent's relationship with the other.
- Magical and egocentric thinking.
- Has imaginary friends.
- Can tolerate lengthier separations from a parent, and enjoy brief separations.
- Takes aggressions out on the parent.
- Vacillates between wanting and demanding attention, or wanting no attention at all.
- May become infatuated with his or her social life.
- May want to be younger, a baby; or, big, strong and "in charge."

Normal Abnormalities and Developmental "Quirks"
When the child is required to attend preschool programs or become involved outside of the family, it is his or her first real periods of separation, and the child may respond very negatively at this time.

If Things Go Wrong
Feels bad about self, low self-esteem, conflicts over responsibility, identity problems, sometimes gender identity problems, grave difficulty with separations.
- Out-of-control behavior or chronic oppositionality.
- A passive and non-spontaneous style of relating.
- Lack of role-taking.
- Approaches strangers, or a clear preference for attention from a stranger.
- Unimaginative, disinterested in play, or emotionally flat.
- Absence of evidence of basic psychological conflicts.

School-aged children (6-11)
A period of mastery, social encounters, peer sensitivity, conscience development, and awareness of strengths and weaknesses all form part of their mental and emotional landscape. They need stability and predictability in primary family relationships, allowing them to gradually expand their social world and to master challenges and situations outside of the care of family. Children of this stage need to continually learn more about themselves and gradually build a sense of identity. Parents must be "islands of security" for the child as he or she ventures out into the world outside of the family. Children must be allowed and supported to take on new activities and trials, to face the inevitable "ups and downs," the gains and losses, as they try on new roles and abilities and check out their "goodness of fit." Parents who are firm, but flexible, are most successful in guiding their children through the roadblocks of middle childhood. The child's introduction to a world outside of the family brings up many insecurities, new challenges, and relationship dilemmas. It is crucial for the parent to tolerate moodiness, strong emotion, "good and bads," and the normal changes and conflicts of this stage.

Normal, Expectable Behavior
- Expanded interest in the social world outside of the family.
- Increased conscience, moral development, and values consonant with family.
- Occasional tantrums are expected.
- Toward end of period, children show more emotional psychological equilibrium.
- Emphasis on mastery and competency.
- Social interactions, primarily with same-sex peers.
- Lessened distractability, increased concentration.
- Greater "controls from within."
- Fairness is an issue.
- Gradually, a movement away from family, with time with friends and special

relationships, secrets and gossip, and concern or social status toward end of stage.

Normal Abnormalities and Developmental "Quirks"
- Fluctuations in mood, attitude, and emotional control.
- Testing limits, and challenges to authority on occasion.
- Crying, painful emotions, and verbal rather than physical outbursts in response to frustrations.
- Day-dreaming, absent-mindedness, forgetfulness.
- Emotional outbursts, mood swings, and occasional explosive behavior.
- In older children, secretive behavior, verbal aggression, and unrealized verbal threats.

If Things Go Wrong
- Disinterest or avoidance of relationships outside of the family.
- Distractability, lack of self-regulation that significantly interferes with learning, or emotional and behavioral control.
- Avoidance of competition, challenges to mastery.
- Lack of curiosity about self, body, physical development
- Premature demands for freedom and individuality, attempts at premature freedoms, parentified and over-controlling behavior.
- Insecurity, worrisomeness, varied immature fears.
- Dependent or 'good child' behavior.
- Tantrums, control battles, resistance to authority, limits, or discipline.
- Lack of knowledge of self, egocentrism, magical thinking.
- Absence of friends, lack of identification with same-sex group or peers.
- Rejection of family values or morals.

Preadolescence/Adolescence: 11-18
With efforts at psychological separation, they seek to develop their own values and sense of identity, intactness, control, and sexuality. During adolescence, the family must provide a secure base for the child's transition to adulthood. The changes necessary during this period often mirror those of their first years. Separation, development of identity, and dealing and integrating losses are psychological tasks that threaten to overwhelm the child. A psychological and emotional "roller-coaster" fortunately is accompanied by periods of relative calm and stability...allowing both parents and child to "recover" before the next onset of change. At no time other than the earliest years does support and availability matter more. Growth during this stage occurs "in opposition," and parents must

be available, supportive and non-rejecting. Expectations, rules, and guidance from parents is necessary if the teen is to gradually and positively take control of self and behavior. During this period, parents should practice "caring control," gradually passing responsibility onto the teen and encouraging their child to assume more control over his or her life. Accordingly, limits must be set in a non-punishing manner, with "limits on limits" and a healthy sense of humor two ingredients for parenting success. Additionally, parents must be able to tolerate the near-constant fluctuations of the teen, with varying demands. While the parent who copes with such vacillations by being increasing rigid and inflexible risks a chronic, conflictual relationship with their teen, the parent who is too allowing, or trusting, or needful of closeness with their teen risks an inability to set limits, impose rules, and necessary control of their teen. In a cruel twist of nature, the precise time in life that teens are challenging, facing issues and growing—with a search for identity— many parents are also entering a period of their own maturational mid-life crises.

Normal, Expectable Behavior

- Issues mirror those of children in their first five years.
- Gradual disengagement from family, to engagement with peers.
- Separation issues, along with identity, identification with and loyalty to peers.
- Dramatic emotional, physical, and cognitive changes.
- Questioning, often painful, of identity, beliefs, and belongingness.
- Widely varying periods in growth, from being annoyed, irritated, angry, and critical, to outgoing, responsive, expansive, and self-assured.
- Able to reason and problem-solve with more sophistication.
- Less reliance on external controls toward internal controls, and more self directed behavior.
- Rejection of family values and rules, while at the same time confusingly embracing family belongingness.
- A return to self-centeredness, and egocentrism and magical thinking.
- Placing needs above those of anyone else.

Normal Abnormalities and Developmental "Quirks"

- Occasional irrationality, unreasonableness, avoidance of consequences.
- Daydreaming, "spaceyness," poor memory, being out of touch.
- Extreme emotional mood swings, inability to delay gratification.
- Acute periods of dependency, avoidance of peers, over-reliance on family.
- Identity confusion.
- Laziness, self-centeredness, inability to set realistic goals and overcome the strength of his or her own inertia.

- Verbal rejection of family values, back-talking, snottiness, sarcasm.
- Self-centeredness, uncaring attitude toward others and possessions.
- Loss and abandonment issues, feeling like does not belong.
- Sexual interest, behavior, and talking, fascination with sexual issues.

If Things Go Wrong

Problems in school and peer relationships, interruptions in mastery and learning, delayed conscience development. If feeling no control, dependency, depression, self-destructive or antisocial behavior. One danger is premature emancipation, an "emotional cut-off" from family and adults, and inappropriately intimate relationships to replace this.

- Drug or alcohol abuse that extend past "normal" experimentation.
- Withdrawal from family, especially if accompanied by withdrawal from friends and peers.
- Depression, emotional flaccidity, inability to feel pleasure.
- Self-destructive thinking, threats, or mirroring acts, signaling suicide thoughts or feelings, or identification with "weird," cultist, or overly hostile/negative philosophies, groups, or peers.
- A drastic drop in grades or in school attendance.
- Runaway behavior, sneaking out, consistent violation of reasonable curfews.
- Risk-taking behavior.
- Identity issues, or adoption of antisocial, avoidant, pseudomature, or immature ways of behaving and coping.

Designing Developmental Interventions: Addressing Failures in Young Children

Self-regulatory Failures

Children with serious regulatory problems, such as eating, sleeping, and potty problems, are easily overwhelmed by stimuli. They show a variety of oddities in coping with sensations and feelings that threaten to overwhelm them, as they cannot understand them.

- Set routines and maintain timing
- Use transitional objects
- Encourage activities that establish body boundaries: interactional games, moving, rocking, jumping, dancing, etc.
- Need to play with them
- Find out what stimulates, overstimulates them

- Use affectionate and less intrusive holding, rocking, tickling, comforting, use humor

Poor Sense of Mastery and Independence
- Devise and choose activities and games child can succeed in
- Praise, reinforce, reward
- Give small challenges, and break down to one effort/undertaking at a time

Affective Flooding/Failure to Emotionally Control
- Help child to use feeling words
- Use "touch talk"
- Speak for the silent child
- Permission to have feelings, model expression
- Interpret and put feeling words to the child's body language
- Stay connected, particularly during negative child emotions—such as anger

Opposition, Defiance, Extreme Resistance
- Set structure and limits
- Set disciplinary techniques
- Parental agreement and consistency
- Enforce limits non-punitively

Poor Imagination, Expressive Problems
- Positive activities and play with the child
- Talk/read with the child
- Incorporate more creative, fantasied, and imagination-oriented activities and play
- Encourage child to take turns and express

Lack of Empathy or Concern for Others:
- Teach give-and-take, mutuality, and problem-solving (simple, like taking turns)
- Emphasize the child's feelings and hurts—specially tune into the child
- Give choices and discuss/reinforce choices
- Teach ways other than physically communicating feelings—'talk, first'

This article is excerpted from Dr. Kunstal's Workshop "Healing Attachment and Relationship Disturbances in Children and Adolescents," presented at the annual NACAC conference, Charlotte, North Carolina, August 2001. It is reprinted here with permission of the author.

invisible
disabilities

HE DOESN'T NEED A
WHEELCHAIR, BUT IT'S THE
ONLY WAY TO SHOW YOU HE
HAS A DISABILITY.
— Sunny Hill Health
    Centre for Children
    Poster Campaign

What Are Invisible Disabilities?

by Sara Graefe

Maybe you've seen him. His picture was plastered on billboards around the province a few months ago. A boy in a wheelchair. The caption read, "He doesn't need a wheelchair but it's the only way to show you he has a disability." It was an ad for B.C.'s Sunny Hill Hospital.

What are invisible disabilities? While not an official medical term, it's an expression that's being tossed around a lot these days, particularly since B.C. Child, Youth and Family Advocate Joyce Preston identified "Children with Invisible Disabilities" in her 1995 annual report as the first of seven pervasive, problematic issues facing children and youth in this province.

An invisible disability is, just as the term suggests, a debilitating condition which is not readily *visible* to the eye. The Sunny Hill ad captures this concept beautifully. Many people tend to make assumptions about others' abilities based on outward appearances. If a child *looks* just like any other child that age, people often expect the child to behave like his/her peers. While they would be willing to accommodate the special needs of a child in a wheelchair, they may be unaware or less supportive of a child who outwardly *looks* like anyone else but who has a "hidden" condition such as FAS or dyslexia.

An Umbrella

Invisible disabilities is not in itself a diagnosis. It's an umbrella term which captures a whole spectrum of hidden disabilities or challenges, which would include NAS, FAS, ADHD, autism, brain injuries, and learning disabilities. As the Advocate reminds us in her report, this list is not intended to be exhaustive, but rather helps identify some of the key groups of people who find themselves elbow to elbow under this large umbrella. Umbrellas are useful because they allow diverse groups of people to come together and define their common denominators in order to form a larger, cohesive group with a stronger voice and more visible presence, which is useful for both raising awareness in the community and for lobbying government.

When grouping people together under "invisible disabilities," there is the recognition that individual conditions or needs may be different, but that those affected face similar misunderstandings and difficulty accessing services because their disabilities are not obvious. As the Advocate outlined in her report.

"Children and youth with [each of] these disabilities have specific service needs. However, the experiences of their families with the health, educational and social service delivery systems, as reported to this office, were remarkably similar. At best, what happens can be described as random - it depends on the attitude and/or knowledge base of the particular individuals and community agencies involved. There is no consistency, no clear ownership, no definition or fixed point of responsibility. Parents end up having to educate service providers in order to access services, a process they describe as exhausting. Often they find themselves blamed for problems and accused of being inadequate parents. This becomes one more thing they have to cope with in an already full and demanding life" (p.28).

Creating Visibility

Sunny Hill Hospital has similarly identified a need to raise awareness about many hidden conditions, and crafted an ad campaign using the invisible disabilities umbrella. This is where the boy in the wheelchair fits in, along with a series of accompanying ads, one which features another child in a wheelchair with a talking computer, and another with a child in Mickey Mouse ears with a slogan about hearing impairment. Sunny Hill offers an "umbrella of services" to match the spectrum of special needs under "invisible disabilities." Because of the hidden nature of these disabilities, Sunny Hill's presence in this field is often invisible as well, at least to the public at large. Chris McBeth, spokesperson from the hospital's public relations office, says that many people don't even know that Sunny Hill exists. As well as raising awareness in a general sense, the ad campaign is intended to inform people that Sunny Hill is out there, and to highlight the different kinds of work that they do. Meanwhile, Chris assures me that the boy who doesn't really need the wheelchair is scheduled to return to the bus shelters and billboards in the near future. So watch for him! And keep in mind that he (or she) is everywhere, every day--in the classroom, in the shopping mall, on the bus, and in your neighborhood.

This article is excerpted from a version that originally appeared in the SNAP newsletter, Vol. 13#1, Spring 1997. © Society of Special Needs Adoptive Parents, 1997

Invisible Disabilities:
A Sampler
by Sara Graefe & Verna Booth

Invisible disabilities is an umbrella term that refers to many different disabling conditions or challenges that are not always obvious—at least at first glance. Talking about invisible disabilities in a broad sense is useful for raising awareness and for advocacy. However, it is also important to recognize and give name to the individual disabilities under the umbrella.

SNAP has compiled a list of examples as a place to start—the material has been pulled from a range of sources and the result is a veritable grab bag. Some of these conditions you have likely encountered before; others may be completely new. While the list is not exhaustive, it attempts at the very least to capture the spectrum of challenges—behavioural, psycho-social, emotional, and physiological—that fall under the term "invisible disabilities." We hope that it will inspire you to consider other possibilities that haven't been listed here. Also, the definitions we've included only skim the surface of each disability. We encourage you to seek out further information on specific areas of interest.

Learning Disabilities

Learning Disabilities (LDs) is a difficult term to define as it is an umbrella expression in itself, referring to a particular subset of invisible disabilities that directly impact behavior and learning. The learning Disabilities Association of Canada adopted the following official definition in 1981:

> Learning disabilities is a generic term that refers to a heterogeneous group of disorders due to identifiable or inferred central nervous system dysfunction. Such disorders may be manifested by delays in early development and/or difficulties in any of the following areas: attention, memory, reasoning, coordination, communicating, reading, writing, spelling, calculation, social competence and emotional maturation.
>
> Learning disabilities are intrinsic to the individual, and may affect learning and behavior in any individual, including those with potentially average, average or above average intelligence.
>
> Learning disabilities are not due primarily to visual, hearing, or motor handicaps; to mental retardation, emotional disturbance, or environmental disadvantage; although they may occur concurrently with any of these.
>
> Learning disabilities may arise from generic variations, biochemical factors, events in the pre-to perinatal period, or any other subsequent events resulting

in neurological impairment.

Language Disorders
Language Disorders are a type of learning disability, and are usually easier to detect in younger children. They are characterized by problems in articulation, expressive language and receptive language--in listening and speaking. *Language delay* is a common symptom. If your child is not saying anything by the age of two, you should bring it to your doctor's attention (Underwood, 1996).

Children with a language disability usually have no difficulty with spontaneous language (situations where one initiates whatever is said). They do, however, often have problems with demand language (where someone else sets up a circumstance in which you must communicate). This inconsistency or confusion in language behavior often puzzles parents and teachers (Silver, 1992).

Speech Disabilities
Speech disabilities are similarly a subset of Learning Disabilities, and are manifested by problems in using words, sentence structure, and style. Children may consistently misenunciate common words and mix up their sentences. These problems may relate to auditory difficulties (Underwood, 1996).

Dyslexia
Dyslexia is one of the most common reading disabilities. Dyslexics frequently reverse letters and words, have difficulty determining left and right, and lack the ability to properly distinguish the sequences of letters and sounds in written words (Underwood, 1996).

Dyscalculia
Dyscalculia is an inability to work with figures—one that runs far deeper than a simple lack of talent. It is a problem with the whole concept and language of mathematics (Underwood, 1996).

Dysgraphia
Dysgraphia is the inability to write legibly, often caused in part by fine motor and perceptual difficulties. In some cases, the child's brain has trouble interpreting what their senses are telling them to do (Underwood, 1996).

Irlen Syndrome
Irlen Syndrome is a perceptual dysfunction that impacts reading and writing activities. Children with Irlen Syndrome put more energy into the reading process

because they are inefficient readers who see the printed page differently than the proficient reader. Constant adaptation from print or from white background causes fatigue and discomfort, while limiting the length of time these children can read and maintain comprehension. Flourescent lighting, glare, high gloss paper, and black/white contrast can intensify symptoms (Irlen Centre, 1996).

The Irlen Centre in Ottawa notes that Irlen Syndrome "is not, of itself, a learning difficulty in the accepted sense." Instead, it is a complex, variable condition that often coexists with other LDs, such as dyslexia, dysgraphia, dyscalculia, ADD, or hyperactivity.

Attention Deficit Disorders

Attention Deficit Hyperactivity Disorder (ADHD) has been called by many names over the years: organic drivenness, "fidgety Phils," post-encephaltic behaviour disorder, minimal brain dysfunction, hyperkinesis, hyperactivity, attention deficit disorder (ADD) with or without hyperactivity. Most of the current literature uses ADD and ADHD interchangeably (Thompson, 1996).

Children and adults with Attention Deficit Disorders (C.H.A.D.D.) Canada defines ADD/ADHD as a treatable medical condition commonly characterized by the presence of inattentiveness and/or hyperactivity and impulsivity at developmentally inappropriate levels. Not everyone with ADD is hyperactive and impulsive. Children with the Predominantly Inattentive form of ADD are generally not impulsive, but have great difficulty with attentiveness and organization. It is estimated that 3 to 55% of the school-aged population have ADD/ADHD. Boys are thought to be about three times more likely to be affected than girls.

Parents may notice symptoms of ADD/ADHD in their children as early as infancy or toddlerhood. Teachers often describe students with ADD/ADHD as being restless, inattentive, easily distracted and overly impulsive. In school, children with ADD/ADHD may have difficulty organizing their work, following instructions, and producing tidy written work. However, when they are particularly interested in something like a movie or video games, they may not appear to have any trouble paying attention (C.H.A.D.D.).

C.H.A.D.D. Canada reminds us that not all children who exhibit these symptoms do so as a result of ADD/ADHD. Disorganized home or school environments, lack of motivation, emotional difficulties, or the existence of other conditions can cause similar symptoms. The difference for children with ADD/ADHD is that the ability to control their behaviour is compromised by the disorder.

Up to 70% of children with ADD/ADHD will continue to show symptoms of the disorder in adulthood. If properly managed, many of the characteristics of childhood ADD/ADHD can be beneficial qualities in adult life (C.H.A.D.D.).

Conduct Disorder

Conduct disorder is a disruptive behavioral problem. It is defined as a persistent pattern of conduct in which the basic rights of others and major age-appropriate societal norms or rules are violated. The behaviour pattern is typically present in the home, at school, with peers, and in the community.

Physical aggression is common. Children or adolescents with this disorder usually initiate aggression, may be physically cruel to other people or to animals, and frequently deliberately destroy other people's property. They may engage in stealing with confrontation of the victim, as in mugging, extortion or armed robbery. At later ages, the physical violence may take the form of rape, assault or, in rare cases, homicide.

Conduct disorders fall into three categories: group, solitary aggressive, and undifferentiated. *Group conduct* disorders are most evident when the person is with peers. *Solitary aggressive conduct disorders* usually manifest themselves as aggressive physical behaviour towards adults or peers but not as function of group or gang activity. The *undifferentiated* type represents a mixture of clinical characteristics.

Conduct disorder problems are often preceded by other problems, including appositional defiant disorder, attention deficit disorder, and family dysfunction (Horne & Sayer, 1990).

Oppositional Defiant Disorder

Oppositional defiant disorder is similarly a behavioural problem, characterized by a pattern of negativistic, hostile and defiant behaviour without the more serious violations of the rights of others that are seen in conduct disorder.

Children with this disorder are commonly argumentative with adults, frequently lose their temper, swear, and are often angry, resentful, and easily annoyed by others. They often actively defy adult requests or rules and deliberately annoy other people. They tend to blame others for their own mistakes or difficulties.

Oppositional defiant disorders are typically evident in the home, but they may or may not be present outside the home, at school, with friends, or in a clinical interview (Horne & Sayer, 1990).

Attachment Disorder

Children develop an *attachment disorder* when they experience a traumatic period during a very young age. This experience may disrupt or inhibit the bonding process or attachment development between the child and his/her parents.

Attachment disorders often occur if the child experiences a change or separation from one or more parents or guardians, suffers from chronic pain, or faces abuse and neglect. These experiences may inhibit a cycle of events that is the foundation of bonding or attachment process (Waller & SNAP, 1995). Children with a severe attachment disorder have never had a successful attachment to anyone. Children with a mild to moderate disorder have had only partial and never truly rewarding attachments in their short lives (Ziegler, 1994).

There are several different symptoms of attachment disorder and a child may display any number of them. These symptoms quite often indicate a lack of conscience, and inability to build and retain a meaningful relationship with others. The following are indicative of attachment problems:

- unable to give or receive affection
- lack of eye contact
- randomly affectionate with strangers
- phoniness--superficial degree of charm and engagement
- socially uninhibited (impulsive)
- cruel to animals and others
- crazy, chronic lying about the obvious
- learning lags
- preoccupied with fire, blood, and gore, poor peer relationships, inappropriately demanding and clingy
- abnormal speech patterns
- self-destructive behaviour

After recognizing and identifying attachment disorder, professionals with adequate knowledge can start to provide a therapy that re-establishes and nurtures the bonding process (Waller & SNAP, 1995).

Autism

Autism is a lifelong disability of the central nervous system that affects social development and language development, and is characterized by specific behaviours. Autism has an early onset, occurring in infancy or childhood. Symptoms may include the following:

Severe Delays in Social Development
unresponsive to people, unresponsive to physical contact, little or no appropriate play with toys, little or no eye contact, prefers to be alone, inappropriate laughter and screaming, strong inappropriate attachment to objects

Severe Communications Impairment
poor understanding of gestures, difficulties with abstract concepts, lacks comprehension of content and timing conversation, focuses on one topic (perseveration), echoes what is said (echolalia), reverses pronouns
Atypical Behaviours
strong resistance to change in routine, self-stimulatory behaviour (rocking, hand flicking, spinning), hyper- or hypo- sensitivity to sight, taste, smell, touch and hearing, unresponsive to words or sounds, distressed by certain sounds/ noises, insensitive to pain, unresponsive to cold or heat, temper tantrums, self-injurious behaviour
Learning Deficits
difficulty relating learned skills from one environment to another (generalizing); uneven learning patterns (poor skills in some areas, but exceptional abilities in others)

In the first two years of life, the symptoms are often masked by developmental milestones. Symptoms vary from person to person and there is a wide spectrum of severity, from mild to very severe. It occurs in approximately 15 out of every 10,000 births. Autism affects four times more males than females.

Although there is no known cure for autism at the present time, world wide research indicates that the best treatment is early, intense intervention. A strong focus on increasing communication skills and promoting integrated education gives people with autism an opportunity to grow to their fullest potential and be valued members of society (Autism Society of British Columbia).

Sensory Defensiveness

Sensory defensiveness refers to the overcultivation of our protective senses, resulting in a "danger" response. A child with sensory defensiveness may appear to be hyperactive, distractible, and exhibiting behaviour problems (Hittle, 1996).

There are different types of sensory defensiveness, with common symptoms related to each of the sensory symptoms.

Tactile defensiveness refers to under or overreaction to touch. Persons with tactile defensiveness avoid being touched by others. They be irritated by certain types of clothing, or may become agitated by people accidentally bumping into them. They may bump into things roughly as a means of seeking sensation. They may dislike certain textures, including food textures.

Gravitational/postural insecurity describes a seemingly irrational fear of change in body position, or of certain types of movement. An affected child may be fearful of having their feet off the ground, for example.

Visual defensiveness denotes over-sensitivity to visual input. A child with visual defensiveness may be oversensitive to light and visually distractible. They may avoid eye contact and startle easily.

Auditory defensiveness is over-sensitivity to auditory input. Children with auditory defensiveness may be fearful of certain noises like vacuums, fire alarms, car motors, and so on. They tend to notice every little sound, such as the refrigerator turning on in another room (Hittle, 1996).

Fetal Alcohol Spectrum Disorder

Fetal Alcohol Spectrum Disorder (FASD) is an umbrella term that encompasses all the conditions related to alcohol exposure. This includes Fetal Alcohol Syndrome (FAS), Partial Fetal Alcohol Syndrome (pFAS), Alcohol Related Neuro-developmental Disorder (ARND) and Alcohol Related Birth Defects (ARBD).

Fetal Alcohol Syndrome (FAS) is a combination of permanent physical and mental birth defects that may develop in individuals whose mothers consumed alcohol during pregnancy. FAS is characterized by central nervous system damage (e.g. brain damage, cognitive and behavioural dysfunction), growth deficiency (e.g. weight and height below normal), and special facial characteristics (e.g. small head circumference, flattened mid-face, sunken nasal bridge.)

FAS is a medical diagnosis that can only be made when a child has signs of abnormalities in each of these three areas. Other physical defects may include malformation of major organs (including heart, kidneys, liver) and other parts of the body (e.g. muscles, genitals, bones). FAS is an organic brain disorder. It is *not* a psychiatric disorder (SNAP, 1997).

In the past, a diagnosis of FAS required confirmation of the mother's alcohol use during pregnancy. This is no longer the case. New criteria published by the U.S. Institute of Medicine in 1996 breaks FAS down into three distinct diagnostic categories: FAS with Confirmed Maternal Alcohol Exposure, and Partial FAS with confirmed Maternal Alcohol Exposure. Two additional categories are used to describe very specific outcomes of prenatal alcohol exposure: Alcohol-Related Birth Defects (ARBD) and Alcohol-Related Neurodevelopmental disorder (ARND).

Previously, the term Partial Fetal Alcohol Syndrome (pFAS) was used to describe an individual with a history of prenatal alcohol exposure, but not manifesting all the physical or behaviour symptoms of FAS (SNAP, 1994). However, this was sometimes misinterpreted as meaning that pFAS was less severe than FAS. While a child designated pFAS does not have all the physical abnormalities of FAS, the cognitive and behaviour characteristics are similar. As a result, pFAS poses similar lifeline challenges (Astley & Clarren, 1995; Clarren, 1996; George, 1993). As the new Institute of Medicine Criteria is adopted in clinical practice, the terms ARBD and ARND will come into more common usage (SNAP, 1997).

FASD is one of the leading causes of preventable birth defects and developmental delay in Canada and the western world. It leads to problems with learning, behaviour, and community living. It is found in all economic and racial groups. Health Canada, based on incidence rates found in the United States, estimates that there are one to two per 1000 children born with FAS in Canada. FAS is irreversible (SNAP, 1997).

Prenatal Drug Exposure

The term *Prenatal Drug Exposure (PDE)* is used to describe children who are exposed to drugs such as cocaine, heroin, methadone, Talwin, Ritalin, Codeine, and Valium before birth. Another term that is often used when describing pre-birth drug exposure is Neonatal Abstinence Syndrome or NAS. Whereas the term PDE is not an individual condition or drug specific, NAS is employed more readily to describe intrauterine exposure to heroin or methadone and the withdrawal symptoms that may appear after birth. The term PDE also comprises alcohol exposure before birth. However, a pregnant mother's alcohol consumption can result in Fetal Alcohol Syndrome (FAS) with its own set of distinctive traits and challenges.

It is difficult to speak in general terms when discussing PDE effects on children as more studies still need to be done to determine long-term effects. Although at present longitudinal studies are largely missing from PDE-based research, recent studies do exist that show differences in learning outcomes between exposed and non-exposed children. However, the reasons for these differences are often not uniquely drug-related. Environmental factors come into play, which add to the impact of the child's drug-intake. Recent studies that deal with physical and neuro-behavioural outcomes in newborns show that prenatal exposure to marijuana, cocaine, and opiates increases the possibility that these children will be born prematurely, weigh less, have smaller heads, and have a shorter stature than unexposed infants.

After birth the child might have a tendency to be jittery and hard to settle. A child who has been exposed to drugs before birth might avert the gaze of a caregiver. These children could experience changes in muscle tone, inhibiting their range of motion and making their movements jerky. It might be difficult for them to relax a hand or foot after stimulation. The parent might notice slightly rapid breathing. At times, feeding can present a problem due to over-stimulation. As the child matures he or she may experience mood swings, tantrums, impaired vision, hyperactivity, speech difficulties, and hearing problems. Some children who are exposed to drugs prenatally may have difficulty building on already-learned skills. They may perform a task one day and forget how to do it the next. These children need prompts and verbal cues to remember.

PDE research shows that effects of prenatal exposure cover the range from severe effects (neurological damage and growth retardation) to minor effects, resulting in normal outcomes. Some studies note that the interaction patterns between the mother and her child, and other social factors, have more effect on some outcomes for children than prenatal drug exposure.

Epilepsy

Epilepsy is a seizure disorder. About 6% of the population in North America will experience a seizure at some point in their lives. However, these are usually single episodes that never recur and do not require medication. Epilepsy refers to individuals with repeated seizures (Batshaw & Perret, 1992).

Epilepsy takes various forms. These include generalized epilepsy, or *grand mal* which is a major fit affecting all the muscles or the body, with a massive contraction followed by a succession of jerky contractions. *Partial seizures* may affect only a few muscles of the body, or may also involve any of the functions of the brain and cause elaborate hallucinations. In *absence attack* or *petit mal seizures*, the affected person, usually a child, is momentarily inaccessible but does not fall or appear to lose consciousness (Collins Dictionary of Medicine, 1992).

Seizure disorders can be treated with medications, a special diet, or surgery. For many children, the seizures are an isolated disability and those affected can lead almost normal lives. For a child with multiple disabilities, the prognosis is generally a function of the other disabilities (Batshaw & Perret, 1992).

Hearing Impairment

Hearing is equalled only by vision among the five senses in its importance to our understanding of the world around us. A hearing deficit is therefore a major disability. *Conductive deafness* results from disorders of the external ear, eardrum, middle ear and acoustical link to the inner ear. *Sensorineural* or *nerve deafness* results from disorders in the inner ear (i.e. a damaged cochlea or acoustic nerve). A hearing loss can range from slight to profound, and may be unilateral or bilateral. Such a loss may exist alone or as part of a multiple disability condition. Defining the type and severity of loss is important for treatment (Batshaw & Perret, 1992; Collins Dictionary of Medicine, 1992).

Often, there is a considerable delay in identifying a child with hearing impairment. It is truly an invisible disability. Infants and young children cannot tell us that they are having difficulty hearing. An early sign of severe hearing loss is a sleeping infant who does not awaken to loud noises. Later signs include lags in meeting developmental speech and language milestones.

fetal alcohol syndrome

OUR LIVES WOULD HAVE BEEN
SO MUCH LESS COMPLICATED IF
ALL THOSE BORN WITH ARBD
(ALCOHOL RELATED BIRTH
DEFECTS) WERE ALSO BORN
WITH FBH (FLUORESCENT BLUE
HAIR).

– Leon's mom

What is FAS?

Fetal Alcohol Spectrum Disorder (FASD) refers to a constellation of physical and mental birth defects that may develop in individuals whose mothers consumed alcohol during pregnancy. It is an organic brain disorder which is characterized by **central nervous system involvement**, **growth retardation**, and **characteristic facial features**.

FAS is a medical diagnosis that can only be made when a child has signs of abnormalities in each of these three areas, plus known or suspected exposure to alcohol prenatally. Other physical defects caused by prenatal exposure to alcohol may include malformation of major organs (including heart, kidneys, liver) and other parts of the body (e.g. muscles, genitals, bones).

FAS is often called a "hidden" or "invisible" disability because its physical characteristics can be subtle and may go unrecognized.

Diagnostic Categories at a Glance
In 1996, the US Institute of Medicine (IOM) published new diagnostic procedures for FAS. Here is an introduction to some of the new terminology. For full diagnostic criteria, please refer to the IOM text *Fetal Alcohol Syndrome: Diagnosis, Epidemiology, Prevention and Treatment* (Eds. Stratton, Howe, & Battaglia), published in 1996 by the National Academy of Sciences.

1. FAS with Confirmed Maternal Alcohol Exposure
A diagnosis is made in this category when there is known, significant prenatal exposure to alcohol and the child exhibits three characteristics:

    i. *growth retardation* (i.e. delayed prenatal and/or postnatal growth)
       This delay must result in height and/or weight very much below normal below the tenth percentile.
    ii. *central nervous system involvement*
       This can result in one or more of the following conditions being observed in the child:

head circumference below the third percentile, developmental delay or intellectual disabilities, and/or other less prevalent conditions.

iii.*characteristic facial features*

These include short eye slits, elongated mid-face, thin upper lip and flattened facial bone structure. These features are most noticeable during early childhood.

2. FAS without Confirmed Maternal Alcohol Exposure

This category is assigned to a child who has the necessary characteristics for a clear diagnosis of FAS, as above, but where there is no way to accurately verify the mother's alcohol use. This new diagnostic category (1996) is helpful for the many children with FAS in foster and adoptive homes, where details about their prenatal histories may be unavailable.

3. Partial FAS with Confirmed Maternal Alcohol Exposure

This applies to a child with a confirmed history of prenatal alcohol exposure who has some, but not all, of the characteristics of FAS. The child does not display all of the characteristic facial features, but exhibits other signs such as growth deficiency, damage to the central nervous system, and/or a complex pattern of behaviour and cognitive abnormalities inconsistent with developmental level and cannot be explained by family background or environment alone. *Partial* does not mean that the condition is less severe than FAS. In fact, Partial FAS can have equally serious implications for education, social functioning and vocational success. Many children diagnosed as Partial FAS would have been designated **FAE ("Fetal Alcohol Effect")** under the old system.

The Institute of Medicine has included two additional categories which are used to describe very specific outcomes of prenatal alcohol exposure:

4. Alcohol-Related Birth Defects (ARBD)

This refers to a child who displays specific physical malformations resulting from confirmed maternal alcohol exposure. These may include heart, skeletal, hearing and visual problems.

5. Alcohol-Related Neurodevelopmental Disorder (ARND)

This applies to a child with a confirmed history of prenatal alcohol exposure who exhibits central nervous system damage as in FAS, inconsistent with developmental level and cannot be explained by family background or environment alone (e.g. learning difficulties, poor impulse control, poor social skills, problems with memory, attention and judgement). As children with disabilities due to prenatal alcohol exposure frequently come from environments where there has been neglect and/or abuse, it can be difficult or impossible to separate which problems are due to alcohol effects and which can be explained by the family living situation. Usually there is a combined effect.

Terminology aside, it is important not to minimize the impact of any alcohol-related birth defect.

Some Common Characteristics at a Glance

No two children with FAS are affected in exactly the same way. However, as a group, children with FAS display more developmental and behavioural problems than other children. The following is a cursory glance at a few common themes which, when coupled with the history of prenatal exposure to alcohol, are strong cues for identification:

- Delays in the development of speech and language, motor skills and social skills in young children.
- Information processing deficits, including the inability to link cause and effect, difficulties generalizing from one situation to another, problems with prioritizing and sequencing, and difficulties grasping abstract concepts, to name but a few. The child may be able to "talk the talk" while unable to "walk the walk"—they may tell you they understand instructions, but are unable to carry them out. They may have learned to *act* as though they understand, but cannot carry through on their own.
- Behavioural deficits in many areas, including interpersonal relationships, communication, daily living skills, sexuality and adaptive skills. These children are often impulsive, hyperactive, easily distracted, have difficulty making transitions, and do not anticipate danger. Older children often exhibit difficulties in the areas of judgement, memory, learning, managing money, and peer relationships. They may have a short attention span, difficulty understanding instructions or following the rules, and poor reasoning ability. They are particularly vulnerable to peer manipulation.
- Abnormal physiological responses, such as a high threshold for pain, no perception of hunger or satiation, difficulty perceiving extreme temperatures, difficulty with visual/spacial perception and balance.

This material has been adapted from SNAP's bestselling book, *Parenting Children Affected by Fetal Alcohol Syndrome: A Guide for Daily Living,* 2nd edition (Ed. Sara Graefe). © 1998 Society of Special Needs Adoptive Parents

Caring for Children with FAS:

Some Day to Day Basics

by Sara Graefe

FAS significantly impairs information processing. This is one of the most devastating characteristics of FAS, since our ability to process information impacts so many areas of our day-to-day lives. And, of course, it makes the task of parenting a child with FAS especially challenging.

For years, families have struggled with the extraordinary demands of parenting children with FAS in isolation, often without knowing the cause of their child's unexplainable behaviour—and frequently being told that the problem is their own poor parenting. Alternate caregivers and educators have been similarly in the dark, baffled by the unusual behaviours and learning patterns displayed by these children—children who are also typically endearing and affectionate, often described as "the cutest child in the class."

Over the years, SNAP has become a leading Canadian FAS resource, essentially out of necessity. FAS has consistently been one of the most prevalent special needs issues faced by our adoptive families—just one of those things that "comes with the territory" in special needs adoption. In our early days, over ten years ago, there just wasn't much out there on FAS for parents, many of whom were only just stumbling on the issue for the first time. We soon discovered that even when armed with information that defined FAS and its characteristics (which does of course provide momentary relief *(whew! At last, a reason for the child's bizarre behaviours!)*, parents were still at a loss as to how to deal with it on a day to day basis.

In 1994, in response to requests from parents and professionals in our community, we first published the manual *Parenting Children Affected by Fetal Alcohol Syndrome: A Guide for Daily Living.* Many of you have told us over the years what a valuable resource this has been, and we have received requests for the book from as far away as Hawaii, the U.K., Africa and Australia. In 1998, we proudly launched the second edition of the guide, fully revised and expanded. This updated, exciting national edition was developed by SNAP in cooperation with the Adoption Council of Canada and with a grant from the Queen Alexandra Foundation for Children. We've revised and expanded all the sections of the original guide to provide the most up-to-date, comprehensive information. Material new to this edition includes the latest Institute of Medicine diagnostic criteria and terms, special considerations for infants and adolescents, parents' needs (caring for the caregiver), and an expanded, national resource list. We're also pleased to announce the publication of the book in French translation, forthcoming later this year, which will bring this important information to French communities in this country.

For those of you who are new to the trenches of FAS, we've excerpted some parenting suggestions as a place to start when grappling with those day to day basics. (If you're a more weathered, battle-weary veteran, you may want to glance through the lists as a refresher—to get some new ideas, or to validate what you're already doing). Based on the input of many parents and professionals, these strategies focus on effective communication and positive parenting.

Please note that this is *not* a definitive list which will always lead to good communication and daily living skills. *Remember that you are the expert on your own child.* You likely know which parenting techniques may or may not work with your child. Keeping individual differences in mind, we invite you to adapt the ideas to suit your children.

Effective Communication

It's important to offer simple directions to children with FAS, and to break down tasks into small steps and teach each through repetition and concrete reward.

- Begin all conversations with the child's name and make eye contact.
- Be specific when telling the child what to do, such as *"sit on that chair"* rather than *"get out of the kitchen,"* and *"hang your coat on the hanger in the closet"* rather than *"put your coat away,"* etc.
- Realize that many words or expressions have more than one meaning and teach these meanings. Children with FAS may be very literal in their understanding.
- Use the same words to express directions for daily routines, such as *"brush your teeth"* rather than *"clean your teeth"* or *"get your teeth done."*
- Be brief and keep directions short. The child may have a short attention span, even though they may appear to be listening. Multi-step directions should be given gradually and only as the child exhibits the ability to follow more complex directions. There is no definite timeline as to when this may occur. For some children, understanding multiple directions may remain a problem throughout their life.
- Give the FAS child separate instructions using their name. The child may not realize that s/he is to follow group-directed instructions.
- Speak slowly and pause between sentences to allow for processing. Auditory processing may lag behind rate of speech. Repeat and restructure information as needed.
- When the child needs to focus on a task or listen to you, you may need to keep

the environment as free from distractions as possible (i.e. TV, radios, video games, other people, etc.) An FM transmitter/receiver (known as a body pack hearing aid) is very useful for screening out distracting noise at school.

- Lists for older children that give step-by-step simple instructions on how to do things can be a useful lifeskill for both common and unexpected situations. Teach the child how to use a list and practice with role-play and simulation games.
- If the child does not know what to do next, jog their memory. Tell, demonstrate, show   and then find a visual way to tap into their memory. If the child cannot remember, remind them and move on.
- Gentle reminders help produce a positive attitude.
- Link one task with another to help establish sequences (e.g. *dinner comes after homework; the bus comes after breakfast; story time comes after the bath.)*
- Use expressive gestures when talking. Try varying loudness, inflection, tone, coupled with hand signals.
- Use as many visual cues as possible to trigger memory and to aid comprehension. Be specific when labelling inappropriate behaviour (e.g. *"John doesn't kick"* with an exaggerated shaking of the head) and include visual cues to emphasize the desired action.
- Touch can be useful for teaching appropriate social distance from others. (E.g. place your hand straight on the child's shoulder and say *"This is where we stand when we stand to talk.")*
- Teach the child a visual or verbal cue to help them understand it is time to begin the task. For example, you might end instructions with the word *"now."* Use exaggerated facial and body language. Use hand signals for behaviour cues with language.
- Help the child interpret social and behavioural cues of others. (E.g. *"That person looks happy because...")* Encourage the child to self monitor and to recognize context, social cues (i.e. facial expressions, tone of voice, posture, etc.) and their own feeling state. Model these skills (e.g. *"How do you think you are (I am) doing right now? Things are getting wild. You (I) need to slow down and take ten deep breaths while doing nothing.")*
- Help the child to express their emotions in acceptable ways.
- Encourage the use of positive self talk: *"I can do this!" "I need to pay attention." "I'm smart!" " I can figure this out!"*
- Help the child develop skills for safe expression of feelings through use of metaphor, art, play, and anger management strategies to provide a bridge to verbalizing issues.

Consequences and Positive Feedback

Processing deficits may make it difficult for the child to connect consequences and feedback to their behaviour. Creating structure in expectations and consequences will aid the child in predicting outcomes and feeling secure in their environment. FAS children may disobey instructions due to lack of comprehension, memory impairment, or—like any child—wilful disobedience. Ask yourself if the child's misbehaviour is due to lack of comprehension or wilful lack of compliance. Recognize your child's unique strengths and weaknesses, build on their abilities and interests, and set realistic goals for performance.

- Often children with language disabilities have difficulty with *"why"*-type questions. Help them learn this format by using alternate forms such as "what is the reason?" or "what caused this to happen?", or restating as *who, what, where, how* and *show me* to invite input.

- Spend time discussing cause and effect relationships. Be patient with their delayed ability to learn this relationship.

- Tell the child what *to* do, not just what not to do. Letting children know what to do gives them a direction to take the behaviour and focuses on the positives while defusing the negatives (e.g. *"Chris, put your feet on the floor, not on the table."*)

- Encourage the child to "help" as a valued member of the family.

- Give immediate rewards or consequences and remind the child what the consequence is for. Parents of children with FAS often notice that rewards lose their effectiveness, and are constantly searching for new ways to motivate behaviour. For some children, stars and stickers on a chart work well, while for others time on the computer or videos is effective. Older children often accept the "cost" for the behaviour (e.g. no telephone privileges or being grounded for breaking curfew) as worth it. The goal may simply become keeping the child out of harm's way.

- Be firm. Set clear, consistent limits. Don't debate or argue over rules. Post family rules in simple words and/or with pictures.

- Separate the child from the behaviour. The action may be *"bad,"* but the child must never feel that s/he is a *"bad"* person.

- When removing a child from a situation to diffuse and calm down, once again separate the child (not a bad child) from the inappropriate behaviour (e.g. *"Your behaviour tells me you need a time-out."*) Always return to the child when calm and reinforce that s/he is a good person.

- Do not issue warnings that you cannot carry out. These children may take you literally. Also, the child learns that there is no consequence when the threat is not carried out.

- Be very specific with praise and criticism. (e.g. *"Joey, good sitting"* or *"Susie, good listening"* with a smile and a touch rather than simply *"Good boy/girl."*)
- Intervene before inappropriate behaviour escalates (this is a difficult thing to do—the caregiver must be tuned into the child's feeling state and behavioural cues *all the time.*)
- Designate a place for "quiet time" when the child feels overwhelmed. Encourage the child to choose a place where s/he will feel comfortable and secure.
- Give the child positive acknowledgement and regard for just being themselves—as well as for desirable behaviour.

Transitions... Things Change
Changes in a child's life, such as moving or starting school, can be traumatic. Children with FAS may also experience difficulty in the simple changes that occur every day, such as moving from one activity to another. This may be the case even when the child is being asked to change their focus from a less pleasant task to a more pleasant one.

For the major changes:
- Develop "hello" and "farewell" rituals between you and your child.
- Use photographs of actual people, places, and important things to prepare a child for   such events as moving to a new home, going to the dentist/doctor, going to the hospital or going to a new school.
- The absence of a family member can be upsetting to the child. Use photographs of the person and the place where they will be to explain their absence.
- If a child must move to a new foster or adoptive home, or is even attending a sleepover, try to keep the child's daily routines as normal as possible. Consistency and routine will minimize negative impact.
- Acknowledge the child's fears about abandonment and other separation issues. Be as reassuring as you can while still being realistic. Help them work through separation issues in advance of an impending move.

For more minor changes:
- Establish routines so that your child can predict coming events.
- Offer structured, limited choices and encourage decision making. Help the child shape their environment.
- Teach the child a visual or verbal cue to help them understand it is time to begin the task.
- Egg timers are a useful way to clearly define the length of an activity.

- Give the child advance warning that an activity will be over soon.
- Prepare the child for school the night before and allow the child to direct as much of this activity as possible. For example, in planning what to wear, offer some limited and structured choices.

Structure and Routines
Build security into the child's day by maintaining consistency. Create a structured environment for children with FAS which includes choices within clear and predictable routines.
- Write down or diagram what needs to be done for the completion of a task. For example, you might post photographs of the child engaged in each step of an activity such as brushing teeth.
- Break down daily activities into specific steps—plan mini-routines within the larger routine. Do everything in the same way and in the same order every day (e.g. wake the child in the same predictable way each morning.) This may help the child be come more comfortable moving between activities, and able to operate more independently.
- Encourage imitation of daily activities through representational play.
- Avoid situations where the child will be overstimulated by people, sound, light or movement.
- Have a place for everything and everything in its place. Allow only one item out at one time if the child is overwhelmed by excessive stimulation. Storing things together by a system (e.g. by type, size, colour, etc.) may assist the child in developing independence within their own environment. For example, if all the blocks are stored together, the child may learn where to go get them without your assistance.
- Place labels on the outside of drawers, cupboards, shelves, and so on. Use single words or pictures to indicate contents.
- If the child has difficulty understanding boundaries and private spaces, such as shared bedrooms, marking off areas with masking tape may be helpful.
- Create a homework corner in a quiet place. Have the minimal but necessary "tools of the trade" there at all times. Use creative language to name this separate, personal space (e.g. the child's *"office," "workshop," "private library,"* etc.)
- Alternate active times with relaxation.
- Help your child to meet children who will be positive role models.

Supervision
Alcohol-affected children may need careful supervision so that they do not get

into trouble or place themselves in dangerous situations. Remember that it is impossible to be everywhere all the time and that structures in the environment can help support supervision. Because children with FAS have trouble understanding the link between behaviour and consequences, they are typically the child in the group who gets caught, even though they may not have been the child who initiated or carried out the action.

- Given that you too must sleep, keeping the child's bedroom fairly sparse can minimize the potential for disaster! For the child who wanders at night, an alarm on the bedroom door may be necessary.
- If the child approaches strangers, deal with it immediately in front of the stranger (e.g. *"This is a stranger, this is someone we do not know. We do not talk to people we do not know."*) This may be difficult and embarrassing, but essential for reinforcing the concept.

Advocacy

The ability to work effectively with schools, doctors and support workers may be challenging but is critical. As a parent, you are likely the best advocate for your own child. Expand your advocacy skills. Look for advocacy resources and workshops in your own community, and check SNAP or your local library for books on self-advocacy.

- Continue learning about FAS. Search out magazines, books, newsletters, movies and tapes for information and support. Attend workshops and conferences. Share your information with professionals involved in your child's life.
- Work beyond the label. Remind yourself and others that a diagnosis of FAS should not be used to label limitations. Each child has different potential. The goal is to facilitate their development so that their fullest potential is realized.
- Recognize that FAS is a relatively new area, and that it will take time for a formal "system" to develop to help affected individuals and their families. Find people who share an interest in the area to work with you and help you through the existing system.
- Join a support group and share your information. Parents in some communities have started FAS-focused self-help groups. Other parents have found much comfort and support in groups for parents/adopted parents of special needs or high risk children. Check your local community resource directory or self-help resource association for listings of groups in your area.
- Find a child advocate if necessary, someone who will champion your cause within a system—be it the school system, the legal system, the medical system or social services. There are formal child advocates within the system, such as the Child, Youth and Family Advocate for the Province of British Co-

lumbia, as well as outside help,
such as community advocacy groups. You can also tap into the support of an "informal" advocate—such as the friend who walks into the principal's office at your side when you lobby for better supports for your child at school.

- Become active in efforts to shape legislation and support research endeavours.
- Make sure you get support for yourself!

This article originally appeared in the SNAP newsletter, Vol. 14 #4, winter 1999. © 1999 Society of Special Needs Adoptive Parents

Special Considerations for Adolescents with FAS

by Sara Graefe

Adolescence is a transitional period from childhood to adulthood. Like any major life transition, it is usually accompanied by crisis. People with FAS often experience many of the same crises as other adolescents—adjusting to sexual maturity, becoming less reliant on parents and family, establishing areas of independence, and planning for a fulfilling role in society as an adult (Streissguth, Ladue & Randels, 1988).

It is often difficult to separate these "typical" teen issues from the disability issues caused by FAS. However, teens with FAS—like those with any developmental disability—have special needs during adolescence.

Parents of a teen with FAS are faced with a range of challenging issues such as:
- sexual maturity in a developmentally disabled person
- their teen's plateauing academic skills and decreasing satisfaction with school, and need for work and social skills
- their teen's high risk for exploitation, peer manipulation, school expulsion and/or involvement in the criminal justice system
- managing their adolescent's leisure time, interpersonal relationships and independence

The following strategies are geared for coping with adolescents with FAS. While these suggestions have been effective with some adolescents, they may not be appropriate for everybody. *As always, remember that your teen is unique. Adapt your strategy to suit their individual needs.*

Structure and Supervision

Streissguth, Ladue & Randels (1988) summarize the best method of coping with adolescents with FAS in three words: "STRUCTURE! STRUCTURE! STRUCTURE!" Parents have the difficult task of finding a balance between permitting freedom appropriate to the child's developmental level, while providing enough structure for protection and growth. Follow your instincts and resist pressure from family members, other adults involved with your child, and the teen him/herself to lessen control and let the teen "learn from their mistakes." The risks are too great.

- Continue to provide a safe, structured environment and clear, predictable routines.
- Clear, consistent expectations and behavioural consequences are still necessary.
- Supervision *cannot* be decreased in adolescence. Although a child may be chronologically fifteen, their mental/emotional functioning may be at a lower level.
- Teens with FAS are easily influenced, and vulnerable to peer manipulation and negative, destructive behaviours such as sex, drugs, alcohol and crime. Carefully monitor social activities and structuring of leisure time. Do not leave alone for an extended period of time.
- Encourage the teen's talents (e.g. music, art, athletics, Special Olympics, etc.) to discourage non-constructive use of leisure time. Identifying strengths and interests is also useful when looking for an appropriate job setting.

Life Skills

As the teen's academic skills plateau, it is important to emphasize work, social and daily living skills. Adolescents need help with day-to-day language skills, interpersonal relationships, managing money, making purchases, looking after their own health, looking after their appearance and clothes, and so on.

- Teach the teen about sex and birth control as you would any hygiene or care issue (i.e. be open, use language and concepts appropriate to the child's developmental age, repeat regularly, seize the teachable moment, have appropriate teaching aids and methods available, etc.) Sex and birth control are important issues for teens with FAS. They have a normal sex drive, which causes problems when coupled with their poor judgement and impulsivity—they are often easy targets for sexual exploitation, both as a victim and a victimizer. Again, supervision is key—like all teens, don't expect that they won't want to try sex just because they've been told not to.
- Children with FAS are at high risk for becoming chemically dependent be-

cause of family histories of alcoholism. Studies show that alcoholism is a disease that is passed on from generation to generation, whether the child lives with the alcoholic parent(s) or not. Adolescents are particularly vulnerable as they are exposed to many more negative influences. Their desire to fit in, coupled by poor judgement and impulsivity, can lead them to substance abuse. Show them alternate ways of having fun, dealing with their feelings, and being accepted by others.

- Help the teen find "sheltered" employment opportunities where the employer under stands that they have hired an individual with a significant disability. The job environment should be one where there is structure, order, and routine, and where the adolescent will be supervised by adults who are patient and understanding of the teen's limitations.
- You may need to accompany your teen to and from work to make sure they get to their destination, or designate someone else to do this.
- Individually structured volunteer placements can help a teen with FAS contribute to the community and develop a sense of participation, accomplishment and responsibility.
- You may always have to "remind" the individual with FAS when things must be paid, even into the adult years. Ideally, establish the routine of paying bills as soon as possible.
- Teens with FAS are susceptible to depression and loneliness. They may be rejected by their peers due to impaired social skills or because they are different. For people who have difficulties making and keeping friends, holding down a job or achieving at school, depression, loneliness and low self-esteem are normal. Psychological counselling is a healthy option to deal with depression and other mental health issues that may arise. It is important to find a counsellor who is experienced working with individuals with FAS or other neurologically-based disabilities.
- Let go of high expectations. Relax about your child's level of achievement and focus on their feelings of self-worth, satisfaction and well-being.

Adolescents with FAS in the Justice System

As children with FAS reach adolescence, they are at increased risk for involvement with the justice system. Their poor judgment, impulsiveness, inability to anticipate consequences, and seeming inability to alter their behaviour as a result of those consequences appears to make them particularly susceptible to trouble with the law. Streissguth et al.'s (1996) follow-up study of adolescents and adults with FAS /FAE found that approximately 60% had experienced some involvement with the law. Forty percent did not!

Teens with FAS/FAE have been charged with offences ranging from vandalism or mischief to more serious offences of theft and assault. They may be easily led and manipulated by more street-wise teens. However, in a recent study in BC., youth with FAS were no more likely to commit the offence with a group than on their own.

Teens with FAS/FAE are also victims. Their inability to anticipate dangerous situations may put them in the wrong place at the wrong time. They may be too trusting of people, including strangers, whom they consider to be "friends". Inappropriate social skills may make them the scapegoats in the teen peer group.

For both perpetrators and victims, alcohol and drug use is often the driving influence.

It is important to remember that having FAS in and of itself does not cause criminal behaviour. Many other factors combine to result in this outcome. The advice to parents to closely monitor their teen's activities is the key factor in preventing involvement with the justice system.

Take Care of You

Respite care is just as important for caregivers of adolescents affected by FAS as it is for parents of younger children. The adolescent years can be particularly exhausting as you are dealing with new stressors on top of the many special needs you have been coping with since infancy and childhood.

This article originally appeared in the SNAP newsletter, Vol. 15 #3, fall 1999. © 1999 Society of Special Needs Adoptive Parents

Revisiting FAS

by Sara Graefe

Life is moving along, and you and your child are growing and changing. You may be weathering the transition from childhood to adolescence, or adolescence to adulthood, and facing a whole new set of issues and challenges. Many of you are battle weary—not only from parenting a child with FAS, but from trying to access many services that still don't exist, and dealing with systems that often don't understand. In spite of everything, you've all made it this far and are carrying on. And it's worthwhile to pause for a moment, to honour yourself for your courage, perseverance and commitment for hanging in there with your child.

For some of you, reading this publication marks the beginning or early stages of your journey—as was adoptive parent Ro de Bree's experience when she opened the SNAP newsletter back in 1990 *(see her article "The Last Orange" on page 61)*. *(see her article "The Last Orange" on page 61)* Perhaps you're hearing about FAS for the first time, or you suspect your child may have FAS, or you've just received a positive diagnosis. This can be a scary time. You're probably experiencing a mixture of relief—finally, a *reason* for your child's behaviour—and a whole range of upsetting emotions.

You might be feeling intense guilt or anger about your child's condition. You are likely anxious about the medical outcome, and worried about future complications and risks. You may be overwhelmed by feelings of helplessness and panic about how to manage the condition, and be anxious about how to plan for the future. Stories from parents who have been down the road before you may make you feel less alone, but can also further the anxiety. You are in a process of grief as you deal with the loss of certain life goals for your child, and come to terms with the necessary changes in living patterns due to the condition. It may be reassuring for you to know that early diagnosis and early intervention are key pieces for reducing the devastating impact of FAS. Armed with today's knowledge, you have a running start on parents who even five to ten years ago were struggling alone in the dark, or for whom information came way too late.

New Developments
In 1996, Health Canada issued a groundbreaking joint statement on the prevention of FAS, co-signed by eighteen national associations representing medical, nursing and midwifery disciplines, aboriginal and multicultural groups, and other organisations known for their extensive work in the area of FAS and other alcohol-related birth defects.

Meanwhile, south of the border, the United States Congress mandated the Institute of Medicine of the National Academy of Sciences to form an international committee to review FAS. This came about in response to confusion around terminology, diagnostic practices, and the disorder itself. A panel of fourteen experts in fields ranging from Pediatrics to Psychiatry—including Dr. Joanne Weinberg, Professor of Anatomy at the University of British Columbia—examined issues including those surrounding diagnostic categories and techniques, the prevalence of FAS and related disorders, and the availability of treatment programs for affected individuals. In 1996, based on the panel's recommendations, the Institute of Medicine published new terminology and diagnostic procedures for FAS, which are now being used in practice.

Dr. Ann Streissguth, a pioneer in the field who heads the Fetal Alcohol and Drug Unit at the University of Washington, published the results of several landmark FAS studies. In 1996, Streissguth and colleagues Bookstein, Barr and Sampson published *The Enduring Effects of Prenatal Alcohol Exposure on Child*

Development (University of Michigan Press), which reports on the results of a study of the systematic effects of prenatal alcohol exposure on 500 children, followed from gestation to seven years. It is the first major longitudinal inquiry, launched soon after FAS was first defined as a medical condition in the early 70s, used to illustrate the long-term effects of alcohol on the mental and physical development of a child. The findings scientifically validate the many difficulties faced by affected children and their families in those first seven years of life.

In 1996, Streissguth, Barr, Kogan and Bookstein released the results of the largest study ever done on people of all ages with FAS and Partial FAS. The report, *Understanding the Occurrence of Secondary Disabilities in Clients with Fetal Alcohol Syndrome and Fetal Alcohol Effects,* examines the type and magnitude of secondary disabilities that are associated with FAS, including mental health problems, disrupted school experience, trouble with the law, confinement, inappropriate sexual behaviour, and alcohol or drug problems. The most important finding was that these devastating secondary conditions *may* be reduced by early diagnosis, appropriate intervention, better understanding, and a stable, nurturing home environment.

The research team followed up with a conference in the Pacific Northwest, which is documented in another great new book, edited by Streissguth and Kanter (University of Washington Press, 1997), *The Challenge of Fetal Alcohol Syndrome: Overcoming Secondary Disabilities.* Twenty-two experts, conference participants from the fields of human services, education, and criminal justice, respond to the secondary disability study with their own recommendations for solutions to the lifelong consequences of FAS.

As if she hasn't been busy enough, Dr. Streissguth released another landmark book in 1997, *Fetal Alcohol Syndrome: A Guide for Families and Communities,* based on her life work in the field. This compassionate book presents an excellent overview of FAS for both parents and professionals, and tackles even the most difficult issues head-on.

Closer to Home
There have also been exciting developments here in BC. Our Provincial FAS/FAE Coordinator outlines recent government initiatives and highlights the burst of community-based activity around the province.

Many SNAP parents have been actively involved in these processes. To name a few, Marjorie Wilson and other members of the Duncan SNAP group are part of the Cowichan Valley FAS/E Action Team who developed the excellent policy brief *FAS and pFAS: Collective Action for Collective Solutions.* Individual parents such as Ro de Bree and Bob Steeves regularly discuss FAS issues in the media, keeping the issue front and centre. SNAP parents and support groups have organized numerous conferences and workshops on FAS over the past few years, in such communities as Maple Ridge, Port Moody, Duncan and MacKenzie.

There have also been small yet significant examples of shifting societal attitudes. As a notable example, the popular Cactus Club Café in Burnaby has taken an innovative approach to FAS prevention. They feature a highly visible warning label directly on their drink menu, presenting the message in a way that's colourful and fun—a goofy picture of the two owners with this message, "Drinking during pregnancy can cause birth defects. But, if you're not pregnant, then check these out!" It's very much in keeping with the young, light-hearted spirit of the restaurant. The message is different; it's eye-catching and harder to "tune-out" than those "no" signs we are so used to seeing everywhere.

SNAP applauds the Cactus Club for their creative approach in tackling this serious issue. Particularly when other businesses still just aren't getting it—West Jet airline being an appalling example, having recently featured an article in their in-flight magazine by a physician who says it's OK for a woman to drink moderately during pregnancy!

Home Grown Publications

There have also been a number of excellent resources recently developed in BC that are worthy of mention. The BC. Ministry of Education Special Programs Branch developed an excellent new manual for classroom teachers, *Teaching Students with Fetal Alcohol Syndrome*, published in 1996. The principal writer on this project is UBC psychologist and SNAP Board member Dr. Julianne Conry. The book provides an excellent introduction to FAS for teachers, and classroom strategies for working with students with FAS. A print copy can be ordered from Crown Publications at (250) 386-4636. The document can also be downloaded from the INTERNET at http://www.est.gov.bc.ca/specialed/fas/title/html.

The B.C. FAS Resource Society received a grant from the Law Foundation of British Columbia to write a book on FAS and the legal system, to provide information about people with FAS to all those working within the legal system—judges and lawyers, as well as police, corrections officials and probation officers. The book is also intended as a resource for FAS-affected individuals who come into contact with the system, as victims, witnesses, or perpetrators, and their families. The book is edited by two well-respected Canadian experts, Dr. Julianne Conry once again, and Dr. Diane Fast, psychiatrist at B.C. Children's Hospital and SNAP Advisory Council member.

Another publication worthy of mention is the moving collection of poems by Leon's Mom, *And Have Not Love* (Metaphor Publishing, 1997), distributed through the Duncan SNAP support group. Leon's Mom started writing poetry in her FAS/ FAE support group as a way of sharing the difficulties of raising teens and young adults with alcohol-related birth defects. Over the years, many of her poems have appeared here in the SNAP newsletter. A selection of nineteen pieces have been put together in this collection to share these experiences more widely, and to increase public awareness. Many parents with alcohol-affected children have found comfort and solace in the immediacy of Leon's Mom's words.

But It's Not Enough

It's great to be able to celebrate our successes. Although FAS continues to have a devastating impact on affected individuals and their families, it is encouraging to that we are moving forward in our knowledge base, prevention, and intervention efforts. As Ro de Bree notes in her editorial, these "small changes keep our hope alive."

But as Carole Legge points out in her piece—and Ro would be the first to agree—there is still so much more that needs to be done. Small changes are *not* enough. While we were compiling this newsletter, another SNAP parent noted, "I don't need any more information—now I just need a solution." It's a sad bottom line.

We now have the hard scientific data to prove what many of us have come to suspect over the years—that early diagnosis and intervention may help reduce the devastating secondary disabilities caused by FAS, and maximize the potential outcome for affected individuals. What we don't have yet are the adequate services to carry this out. Even here in B.C., where we are the envy of many other provinces because of our available services and resources, we are still stuck with long waitlists for diagnosis, fragmented programs which do not reach all affected individuals in need of support, and inadequate services for youth and adults.

What's it going to take for this to change? The facts are clearer than ever; there is no longer any excuse *not* to implement needed services and supports. Government and systems crying poor is simply not good enough. The costs for neglecting adequate prevention and intervention efforts are far too high—for the affected individuals themselves, and for society at large.

It is our hope that in another four years, we will be able to look back and see some vast improvements on this front. But it will not be possible without a coordinated effort between governments, service providers, the medical profession and other "systems" (i.e. education, justice and social services), affected individuals and their families, and society at large.

A daunting task. But that has not stopped us before. I'm sure many of you are thinking, *"but I'm so tired…."* Of course you are. It's vastly unfair that it's always up to you, parents and professionals on the front lines, to keep up the good fight, when simply caring for an individual with FAS is a stressful, exhausting full-time job. But it's your voice that keeps society accountable, and has helped us progress as far as we have today. Take care of yourself, and keep hanging in there. Let's celebrate our progress, and keep rising to the challenge.

This article originally appeared in the SNAP newsletter, Vol. 14 #4, winter 1999. © 1999 Society of Special Needs Adoptive Parents

The Last Orange:
An Adoptive Parent's Perspective
by Ro de Bree

My husband and I joined the Society of Special Needs Adoptive Parents through the back door. We found an advertisement in a local paper, wrote to the old SNAP address (88th Avenue in Delta), and asked for more information. At that time we thought we had only one special needs child, a birth son already diagnosed, but we also had three adopted children. That, in my opinion, fulfilled all criteria for SNAP membership.

Our very first copy of *Families Forever* (now the SNAP *Newsletter*) was a devastating wake-up call. It was the Winter of 1990 edition, focusing on Fetal Alcohol Syndrome. We had already heard about this condition, and had dismissed the possibility; reading Jan Lutke's *Fetal Alcohol Syndrome: A Layman's Guide* made us realize that we were actually living with FAS. Suddenly, there were scary reasons for the bizarre behaviours we had assumed to be the result of "poor parenting."

Since then, we have talked with many older adoptive parents who, through T.V. documentaries or newspaper articles, were finally able to understand their very complicated children. For most of us, the knowledge was too little, and it came too late. For today's adoptive parents, who know what they are dealing with, early diagnosis and early intervention bring lots more hope for the future.

As Good As It Gets
Twenty years ago, when our oldest turned ten, we thought, "This is just a stage...." But it wasn't. And, "she'll grow out of it...", but of course she couldn't, and "everyone learns social skills...eventually." You bet. We didn't understand that we were at that point, in the middle of our very best time as a family—that this

was as good as it was ever going to get.

Instead, we searched for a magic formula. There had to be something we could change—one more course to take, one more behaviour modification technique to try, even a particular phrase that, used often enough, would "fix it." But time moved on, and nothing changed for the better. Our final hope—that maturity would bring improvement—was shattered when we realized that maturity was never going to happen for our three special kids. "Teaching him/her a lesson" doesn't work for most of these individuals; they do not "learn from this experience." They repeat the same mistakes over and over again. It's safer and more freeing to hope for changes in our children's environments than to hope for changes in our children.

Deja Vu All Over Again

In 1996, our family celebrated Christmas on the feast of St. Nicholaas. We expected one of our boys to be in jail by Christmas Day, as he had been arrested and charged the previous September, and we wanted to have one last "family function" together. His case was held over twice. On January 14 he received a conditional sentence. In 1998, we once again called the family together for St. Nicholaas. The same son had committed the same crime, in September, as before, and we anticipated visiting him in jail on Christmas Day. But his case was held over, twice, and on January 12, he received another conditional sentence. Neither his behaviours, nor his timing, have changed. *Our children won't be changing.*

What *CAN* Change

But their environments can change, and our hope is for an educated public. There has been major growth in community awareness, and in media support, in our town during the last few years. Also, along with improved knowledge and better understanding, a noticeable shifting of position has occurred among professionals in governmental systems. In some instances, even the governmental systems have changed.

When my son first became active in the legal system as a juvenile, and in corrections, his lawyer dismissed me with, "And what are you? His mother?"

But now, although my son still counts on Legal Aid, he has a lawyer who connects with his parents, understands his special needs, and is able to push the right buttons for him in the courtroom. His Probation Officer keeps in touch, even when my son is not on probation; those two have developed a friendly relationship unheard of six years ago. The P.O. also encourages my involvement— this is always a surprise, as my son is twenty-three.

And in the courts, there is now a recognition of FAS as a factor in sentencing. Last week, my son appeared before a Judge who said, "A jail sentence, although not unreasonable, will not meet the needs of either this offender or the community." Five years ago, while sentencing my son to yet another three month jail term, the Judge indicated that F.A.S. was just an excuse to go out and do more crime.

The Last Orange

We came to the last Christmas orange in the box; it was a large one, and exceptionally bright and shiny. Knowing that he would have skipped breakfast, I took it to court for my son.

He was waiting for me at the far end of the hall. Our courthouse hallway is the longest, drabbest, bleakest bit of Canadian taxpayer owned real-estate imaginable. Nothing could be more depressing than that hallway; nothing more dismal than the dreary, unhappy Canadians inhabiting it.

I had the orange in my hand. As I walked towards my son, it glowed, and it caught the glance of many. Their eyes followed it. Some of them even smiled.

Small changes keep our hope alive.

This article originally appeared in the SNAP newsletter, Vol. 14 #4, winter 1999. © 1999 Society of Special Needs Adoptive Parents

Isaac's Story:
An Adopted Person's Perspective
by Isaac de Bree

My life started on October 25, 1976 in Victoria, BC. I stayed with my birth family till I was 18 months at which time I was brought into a loving foster home. This wonderful and caring family kept me for six months after which time the court ruled that I could stay for another six months. I was well taken care of and loved by my foster parents and three older brothers and older sister and other foster kids that came for short stays. When my six months was up the court ruled again that my foster parents could keep me for another six months. With this ruling I became a permanent ward which meant that they could adopt me if they chose to. I loved being there and they loved having me. I played with my siblings all the time and let's say things couldn't be better.

But then things got messy for all of us because my biological uncle and aunt wanted to adopt me. At this time I was four years old and I was used to this loving family and did not remember my biological family at all. So visits were planned but I hated the visits because they weren't what I was used to and I refused to go. I sat in my room and said no. My uncle and aunt tried to talk me into it but I wouldn't move. This led them to cancelling their adoption application. But we stayed in contact with cards, letters and photographs and finally when I was 12 my foster parents finished the adoption papers and I could be theirs and everyone was happy.

Everything went well until I was about 17 years of age at which time my uncle and aunt resurfaced with cousins around my age so visits were planned again. I got to meet all my family which was a very big family. During this time I would visit them on a regular basis and tell my adopted family all the good times I had which annoyed them extremely which at that time I didn't understand but now I do. They loved me and thought of me as theirs and I was going to my other family. This now makes sense to me and I kind of betrayed them but they still love me and I loved them. In closing this part of my life I must apologize for any pain I inflicted upon their good name or feelings.

In the next part of my life story I will explain about my schooling. I was let's say a slow learner and did kindergarten twice and the rest of my elementary years were let's say harder than the average student. I had to have homework notes that my mom had to ask for as soon as I got home or I would lose them or forget to do my homework. My mom was always behind me to do my homework and chores before I got to play with my brothers and friends which I found annoying then but now I'm glad. I did especially well with teachers that spent a long time with me and of course my mom being behind me at home to support me. Having less distractions visually and less students in class also helped me. So my advice would be to have good home support, teachers/aids, smaller classes and visual aids and homework notes and a good filing system at home to keep reports and assignments in for future reference.

Getting along with other students wasn't really hard for me in school. I always had good friends that would help me when needed and never did pick on me for being a slow learner. I think it is important no one gets picked on in school and being involved in extra sports and band activities. I spent six years in band class and five years in track and field and cross-country running which I thoroughly enjoyed and was good at. Everyone seemed to enjoy my team approach and sense of humour which I have lost over the years to some extent.

Next I will share my involvement in community activities such as air cadets, boy scouts, altar serving and summer camps. Ever since I was five I have been involved in community organizations. All were enjoyed by me and I learned a lot, especially team work and serving my community in many ways which I am very proud of. I actually won an award one year for doing volunteer work through the scout program. It felt really good to be recognized. For the last 2 years I have been involved in my community by doing education about Fetal Alcohol Syndrome and helping out in other ways to make our community "FAS Friendly" which it wasn't when I was growing up. I can happily say now it is changing thanks to my mom and other wonderful and concerned people. A big thank you to all of them. I really enjoy doing this kind of work and my hope is to make life easier for anyone with FAS and their families by sharing my life experiences. Some paid work for myself would be nice but I think it is more important that people learn about FAS and be supportive of those living with it so they can achieve their greatest potential in life. It takes time and patience but is definitely worth it in the long run. At this time I would like to thank my family especially my parents for doing a really good job for keeping me busy and giving me tools to deal with my past, present and future.

Family life is my next topic. I grew up in a small community with lots of family time. We have a family that has stayed close through good and bad times. Each time one of us would go through a rough time we could count on others in the family to support us. We all know that we would all be there if we could and even the distance couldn't stop us from contact through the phone, letters and emails. We all appreciate the times when we are together again. As a family we all took part in family chores which included raising animals as well as growing our own vegetables. Plus we helped with grocery shopping and household chores. We learned a lot so thanks mom and dad.

In July 14, 1998 I became a dad to Britney which means a lot to me and always will even though distance is a barrier to our relationship at this point. I still stay in contact with Britney's mom via mail, phone and email as the rest of my family does as well.

In closing I would like to thank everyone that has touched and helped my life become the way it is now.

This article originally appeared in the SNAP newsmagazine, Vol.18#1, January/February 2002. © 2002 Society of Special Needs Adoptive Parents

prenatal drug exposure

A LOT OF PDE IS EMOTIONAL,
NOT SO MUCH PHYSICAL OR
MENTAL AS WITH FAS.
> – Shirley Binder

What is PDE?

Facts & Intervention Strategies

by Lissa Cowan and Jennifer Lee

Many children in need of foster and adoptive homes come into care when parents with substance abuse issues aren't able to adequately care for them. Several substances that mothers ingest can hurt infants still growing inside them; these toxic substances take the form of illicit drugs like cocaine and heroin, or licit drugs like tobacco and prescription drugs. Some of these substances result in short term affects after birth, while others last longer.

Poor nutrition and lack of prenatal care can also have a negative influence. Due to the complex nature of a child's circumstances, it's often hard to determine the outcome of prenatal drug exposure on child growth and development. In many cases, pregnant women are multi-drug users. For this reason, the symptoms and behaviours that children demonstrate are very difficult to link to specific drugs. Recent research which focuses on a larger number of children, multiple drugs (including alcohol), and takes into account the child's socio-economic setting has found that many of these children are able to overcome initial challenges that may be related to prenatal drug exposure.

Researchers have yet to explore in depth the extent to which prenatal substance exposure affects behavioural development. Although biological vulnerabilities may be found to exist in children who have been exposed to drugs before birth, many other developmental influences come into play. The impact on a child of an unstable home environment, and poor pre- and post-natal nutrition and care make it difficult to link behaviours to drugs alone.

General Characteristics
- Birth to fifteen months
- Erratic sleeping patterns
- Feeding difficulties
- Irritability
- Impeded language and motor development

Toddlers from sixteen months to thirty-six months
- Atypical social interactions
- Minimal range of play approaches

Preschool children from age three to five
- Hyperactivity
- Short attention span
- Mood swings
- Problems transitioning

School and teenage years

There is insufficient research into the long-term effects of drug exposure on this age range. However, current studies suggest that children who fall into the above categories are at greater risk of developing learning disabilities, experiencing abuse and neglect, and having behavioural problems later on.

Associated Special Needs

Some children who have been drug-exposed prenatally appear to experience few long-term consequences while others suffer more lasting effects. A few recent studies we looked at showed that drug-exposed children are more likely than non-drug exposed children to require medical attention for severe and chronic conditions. These children may also have difficulty forming attachments, and in developing appropriate emotional responses, and coping mechanisms. The following is a list of chief disorders that can be associated with PDE.

- Attachment Issues
- ADD/ADHD
- Learning Difficulties
- Sensory Integration Dysfunction
- Failure to Thrive (FTT)
- Sudden Infant Death Syndrome (SIDS)
- Fetal Alcohol Syndrome (FAS)
- Risk of HIV and AIDS, and other STDs

Caring for the PDE-affected Infant

There has been a lot of controversy in the last few years about the impact of specific strategies on infants born with PDE, particularly relating to those infants who are going through withdrawal as a result of prenatal opiate (e.g. heroin) exposure. Recent research has suggested that many children with PDE have developmental, attachment and attention difficulties because of certain kinds of infant withdrawal treatment, not as a result of PDE itself.

Children who have been prenatally exposed to drugs often have a lower tolerance for stimulation. Infants may cry, stiffen up, appear unresponsive to their caregivers or show signs of distress. For caregivers, the key is to pay attention to the reactions that each kind of stimulation elicits and to counteract the over-arousal before the reaction intensifies. Learn which signs of distress lead to more intense reactions. And, whenever possible, control the kind of stimulation the child is getting. For instance, if the baby has difficulty with loud, continuous noise, make sure that he or she is in another room when the rest of the family is watching an action movie. Also, be particularly alert when leaving the home and going to another environment where you can't control the surroundings.

Comforting Techniques
- Swaddling in soft cloth or blanket
- Gentle rocking
- Warm bath
- Low lighting

Infants with PDE will often have difficulty eating, particularly when they are born premature, underweight or with stimulation control difficulties. They may have difficulty with sucking effectively and gas. The key is to encourage eating without force feeding and allowing the baby as much time as he or she needs to eat fully.

Feeding Techniques
- Feed and burp infant in a semi-upright position
- Feed for shorter periods more frequently

Some caregivers may find that their infants with PDE need to sleep a lot. Others may find that their infants hardly seem to sleep at all! By addressing your infant's stimulation control needs, you will also be helping with his or her sleeping difficulties. The main purpose of your infant's bedroom is for sleeping, so make sure that it's a soothing environment. Avoid bright colours and jarring toys like mobiles or crib-side toys with noise-makers, mirrors or bright colours.

Sleeping Techniques
- Let infant sleep as long as he or she needs to
- Keep bedroom quiet
- Establish a sleeping routine

Current research indicates that after withdrawal and other symptoms specific to infancy, preschool-aged and older children living in supportive homes often display no developmental or behavioural problems associated with PDE.

However, some research still suggests that older children will have difficulties with language and motor skill development, attention and learning, areas that you will have to address individually.

Facing the Big Unknown:
Parenting Adopted Children with Prenatal Drug Exposure
by Sara Graefe

It's been five years now since SNAP first put out a newsletter on NAS (Neonatal Abstinence Syndrome), in which we focused primarily on caring for infants going through withdrawal, and intervention strategies for drug-exposed children. We felt it was high time to revisit the terrain—many of our adoptive parents are dealing with children prenatally exposed to drugs, often in combination with FAS (Fetal Alcohol Syndrome), and are now asking questions about long-term effects as their children grow up.

Mixed Messages

SNAP's first NAS newsletter—along with our popular information package on the topic, compiled by Andrea Daley and Verna Booth in late 1993—appeared at a time when so-called "drug babies" and "crack kids" were sensational news items *du jour* in the popular media. These children were characterized as kids without hope, "walking time bombs" sentenced to a future of chronic failure and crime. It's important to place these reports in context: crack first hit the streets in a big way in the mid-eighties, and the ensuing media furor of the early nineties coincided with the first wave of crack-exposed children hitting an inadequately prepared public school system.

Since that time, there have been notable shifts in perceptions and research findings. Recent studies suggest that while prenatal substance exposure cannot be "reversed," environment can have significant impact (Edelstein, 1995; Barth & Needell, 1996). Most recently, Training, Intervention, Education and Services to support the adoption of substance-exposed children (TIES) reported findings that prenatally exposed children can blossom and even *thrive* in a stable, structured adoptive home environment where the family receives outside support (1999).

This is certainly good news for adoptive parents. However, findings such as these have also sent the media scrambling to the other extreme, dismissing the earlier hype as a hoax and broadcasting blanket statements such as: "Drug Babies Doing OK" and "Little Lasting Harm for 'Crack' Children"—minimizing the very real challenges parents continue to face with their drug-exposed children (which in fact continue to be acknowledged in the same studies cited above).

Long-Term Effects?

So, what's the real scoop? What are the long-term effects of exposure to drugs *in utero*? What happens when these children grow up? As I mentioned above, we're asked this at SNAP all the time—as are the good folks at YWCA Crabtree Corner and Sunny Hill Hospital, who also provide services for drug exposed children and their families.

It turns out that little is actually known about the long-term biological effects of prenatal drug exposure (Edelstein, 1995; Richardson, Hamel et. al., 1999). Here are some reasons why:

1. Prenatal drug exposure is a relatively new area of concern, and it will take time for a substantive body of research to occur, and for a formal "system" to develop to help affected individuals and their families (more is currently known about FAS, which itself was only formally defined as a syndrome twenty-seven years ago).

- Experts such as Edelstein (1995) point to the need for longitudinal prospective studies—studies that follow the same group of exposed children through childhood and adolescence—to build a solid base of pertinent knowledge. The first wave of such studies started in the early 1990s, and those children are now only just reaching late childhood. We'll have to see what lies ahead as the researchers follow these same groups of kids through adolescence—which doesn't help you much now as your own drug-exposed child grows up. But bear in mind that your experience with your child will contribute to the ever-growing knowledge base, helping to identify service needs for yourselves and for future generations.

2. While there has been growing research in this area over the past fifteen to twenty years, it remains difficult to draw conclusive evidence as the studies themselves have produced conflicting results. Experts attribute the difference in findings to a whole host of methodological problems involved in studying the effects of prenatal drug abuse. For example:

- Many studies have used samples that are not representative of the general population of pregnant drug users (selecting subjects from prenatal drug treatment programs, or at delivery based on a positive urine test, or based on lack of prenatal care).

- Accurate measurement of substance use in pregnant women is a difficult task. Many women are unwilling or hesitant to report their usage. Further, many women change their pattern of substance use as their pregnancy progresses.

- Many women's drug use is accompanied by use of other substances, such as tobacco, other drugs, and alcohol—how does one begin to separate the effects of these various substances? What's a manifestation of FAS, and what's NAS? Does the mixing of these drugs have its own impact, as the fetus swims in a veritable chemical soup?

- Many studies on long-term outcomes have focused on samples of children who remain in the birth family. Parental substance abuse is often associated with poverty, homelessness, violence, child abuse and/or neglect—environmental factors which can also significantly impact a child's development.

- Studies which have focused on drug-exposed children in stable adoptive families, on the other hand, may help us separate biological from environmental impact. However, researchers who've studied affected adoptive children also point out the difficulty separating the impact that significant adoption issues have on the child's development and behaviour—such as attachment, grief and loss, a history of trauma, abuse and/or neglect—from the possible long term effects of prenatal drug exposure.

What We Do Know
The effects of drug exposure are not predictable. Some children are significantly affected while others with apparently similar exposure seem to experience few or no consequences.

- Infants exposed prenatally to drugs and alcohol are more likely to have difficulty with muscle tone, more difficulty becoming oriented to their environment (such as following the parent's gaze), and more difficulty regulating their behavioural state (such as moving from a sleeping state to a waking state). These babies tend to be easily overstimulated (and highly irritable when overstimulated).

- Affected children who exhibit language delays, distractibility, and/or problems with fine motor coordination during the preschool period are at increased risk for learning disabilities during their school and teenage years (Edelstein, 1995).

- Behaviour problems affect about a third of children exposed to drugs in the womb, and are similar developmentally to the problems experienced by infants: difficulty concentrating, difficulty staying on task, and increased distractibility. Some children also have aggressive or impulsive behaviour, which can also affect self-esteem and school performance. They can have trouble with attention, arousal (easily overstimulated), and affect regulation (They can have long temper tantrums and may have trouble pulling themselves together after an outburst without the help of the caregiver). Adoptive parents in the TIES study (1999) also reported that their children experienced eating struggles and difficulty adapting to change.

- Attachment problems have been reported by adoptive parents of drug-affected children. The child may have indiscriminate and superficial relationships with other adults. Parents often report difficulties with bonding and feeling close to the child (TIES, 1999).

- The child's number of placements and moves prior to adoption seems to have a greater impact on both the outcome for the child (and the success of the adoption) than prenatal drug exposure (Barth & Needell, 1996; TIES, 1999).

What Does This Mean?
There is hope for drug-exposed children. They aren't the out-of-control monster kids that were once portrayed in the popular media. Does this mean you can now brush the whole thing off with a, *"Phew! No problem?"*

Certainly, the recent findings on environment such as the TIES adoption study provide reassuring news for adoptive families. So let yourself breathe a well-earned sigh of relief, but at the same time, *don't lose sight of the potential problems—and ensuing challenges—*listed above. As the media sways the other way with its reports of these kids being "no risk," it becomes increasingly easy for others to minimize or deny the effects of prenatal drug exposure on your child — and for you to feel like a "bad parent" if your child is having problems.

Keep in mind that while the TIES study shows that drug-exposed children can thrive in adoptive homes, it also reported that adoptive parents found raising these kids both more rewarding *and* more difficult than they had imagined (a paradox, I might add, that many of you know so well!).

Clinical social worker Susan Edelstein, who was involved in the TIES study, has worked extensively with prospective adoptive parents to prepare them for the challenges of taking on children with prenatal substance exposure. In her groundbreaking book, *Children with Prenatal Alcohol and/or Other Drug Exposure: Weighing the Risks of Adoption* (1995), she recommends that adoptive parents walk a middle road in the face of the mixed information and the big unknowns. It's important to keep the focus on best meeting your child's needs, without overemphasizing or denying the child's potential (or actual) difficulties:

Go into the adoption with your eyes open. While there are no guarantees about the outcome of *any* adoption—just as there are no guarantees regarding a child's future in the birth family—keep in mind that there are unique uncertainties and ambiguities inherent in adopting children prenatally exposed to substances. (Note that even those professionals and researchers who emphasize the positive benefits of a stable environment *also* agree that prenatal exposure to drugs is detrimental and should be avoided if at all possible.) As an adoptive parent, you must be willing to tolerate living with the unknown, and prepared to deal with problems should they arise.

Maintain an attitude of realistic optimism: hope that your child will be spared serious consequences, but accept the probability that some preventative and/or remedial interventions may be necessary, and that professional guidance may also be required at such times. As Edelstein points out, "such an attitude is quite different from one holding either that the children are 'doomed' or that they are 'just fine.'"

Don't freak out: extreme media reports and labels that make sweeping, often inappropriate generalizations about your child can be upsetting. Try not to let these messages overwhelm you. Remember that you know your child best.

Work with identifiable problems. Whatever behavioural symptoms a child may demonstrate in the school system (and whatever their cause), the child can be assessed for both learning strengths and problems. A team of teachers, psychologists, speech and language therapists, hearing and vision specialists, nurses, and other professionals can assess difficulties with learning that may be related to short attention span, speech and language problems, impulsivity, short-term memory difficulties, auditory and visual processing, etc. Parents and professionals can then work together to develop an Individual Education Plan (I.E.P.) to help the child or adolescent compensate for the identified problems.

Put primary intervention strategies in place. Edelstein suggests that professional and adoptive parents can:

• Advocate for specialized educational services within the school system, tutoring for academic underachievement, and assessment and intervention for neuropsychological problems

- Explore recreational and work experiences that will give school-age children or adolescents the opportunity to experience success.
- Participate in parent support groups that provide education and guidance for dealing with difficult childhood and adolescent behaviours.
- Participate in individual and family therapy.

Other Things You Can Do

Structure your child's environment. All children benefit from the security of everyday structure and consistency in the home. Create a structured environment for your drug-exposed child which includes choices within a predictable routine—this can help lessen some of the problems related to self-regulatory behaviour and disorganization which many substance-affected children experience.

Stay informed. Keep up-to-date on the new research in this field, and stay abreast of the latest information about the effects of prenatal substance exposure on children. Search out magazines, books, newsletters, movies, videos and audio-tapes for information and support. Attend workshops and conferences. Discuss your questions and concerns with your social worker. Share your information with other professionals involved in your child's life.

Advocate for services on behalf of your children and your family, based on your child's current level of functioning and needs. These might include speech therapy, counselling, special education, respite care, behaviour modification, and/or medical services. Draw upon all resources available to you—including family, friends, community networks, professionals, and support groups. It's also important to access adoption-specific services, where available, to help you understand your child's behaviour in the context of their previous experiences—not only their prenatal exposure to substances, but also grief and loss surrounding adoption, previous trauma, abuse and neglect, etc.

Share your stories and experiences with others. Remember that your experiences with your child are building a broader knowledge base that will help create more effective service and support systems for you and your child, and for others in the future.

Take care of you. Parenting can be challenging even at the best of times. As the adoptive parents in the TIES study remind us, parenting a substance-exposed child can be even more demanding, frustrating and exhausting than you might have imagined. As a parent, it's important not to lose sight of your *own* needs— those things that get lost or overlooked when you're preoccupied with meeting your child's special needs on a day-to-day basis. Get adequate sleep and exercise. Develop a repertoire of stress reduction strategies that work for you. Nurture yourself. Arrange for respite so that you can take time away for yourself on a regular basis to recharge your batteries. Get support for your issues and feelings. Remember that taking good care of yourself is a crucial part of your job. After all, you are probably the most important person in your child's world. How can you effectively support your child if you burn out yourself?

Hang In There

Keep hanging in there with your drug-exposed child, even in the face of the unknown, often daunting future. Hang on to the positives—that drug-exposed children are *not* the demons or write-offs or ticking time bombs portrayed by the media in the past. While these children are indeed at risk, they also possess considerable potential. In spite of the challenges you might face together, you are providing a drug-exposed child a caring, consistent, stable home environment, and in doing so, giving that child the opportunity to grow and be their very best.

This article originally appeared in the SNAP newsletter, Vol. 16 #1, spring 2000. © 2000 Society of Special Needs Adoptive Parents

Living in the Moment:
An Adoptive Parent's Perspective on NAS
by Francine Bruce

We adopted our son, who was diagnosed NAS/FAE at the age of two and a half years old. I remember a day when I had feelings of disappointment and fear. We were adjusting to our "new" son who was *very*, *very* active, and I was telling myself that he needed time too; it was a big adjustment for him as well... I so desperately wanted to just have him be still, so I could hold him in my arms and gaze at him, the way all "new" mothers do!

I could not, and I was disappointed. I was afraid we had made a huge mistake. I prayed to God to help me find a way to get close to this bundle of energy and constant motion. He answered my prayers: our son is now nine and a half years old, and everyday, I can hold him in my arms and gaze at him! It was a long, slow, and sometimes very painful process, but let me tell you, it was worth every tear I have shed.

My son's strength and willingness and his "ability" to forget the "bad" days and begin each new one with love and a song in his heart, is where we question whether his NAS/FAE is a disability or a gift.

How many of us go through life holding onto yesterday's problems, dragging them into today's, and complaining about tomorrow's? Our son has taught us to live each day as a *new* one, and each hour as it unfolds, not because he knows how precious life is or how little time we really have here—but because, for a child with NAS, the mistakes and complexities of one whole day are enormous! It's not easy living in a world that meshes one day into the next, when all you want to do is live for now, for this very moment... But with patience and under-standing, and a willingness to enter into a world where everyday the slate is wiped clean, our son has flourished.

He cannot always understand why he does the things he does. He often gets frustrated and easily angered. He still gets hyper and out of control at times. But he *always* looks at each new day as a wonderful opportunity to be the kind, gentle, caring, thoughtful, funny loving boy that he *is*! I can only say, I wish there were more people like him! Thank you Lord for allowing me to be his mother.

This article originally appeared in the SNAP newsletter, Vol. 16 #1, spring 2000. © 2000 Society of Special Needs Adoptive Parents

adhd

THE BABYSITTER REPORTED
THAT THE KIDS HAD GOTTEN SO
WILD THAT SHE HAD TO CALL IN
REINFORCEMENTS (THREE
ADULTS TO ONE CHILD) TO
BETTER THE ODDS.

– Carol Fyfe-Wilson

Strategies for the ADHD Child

by Stacey Burnard

Attention-Deficit Hyperactivity Disorder (ADHD) is a neurologically based disorder caused by a deficiency of a particular neurotransmitter. It affects approximately 5% of the student population. There are no formal tests but diagnosis is based on clinical history as ADHD is present since early life.

In school, these children often fail to pay attention to details, are easily distracted, have difficulty listening to instructions and initiating or completing tasks, have difficulty with change (moving from one activity to the next) and with organizing (losing/forgetting) things, and are reluctant to work for sustained periods of time; they are constantly on the go. Sound familiar? Regardless of setting, home or school, the behavioural manifestations of ADHD are the same.

The defining characteristics include hyperactivity and impulsivity, which translate into fidgeting and restlessness, blurting out answers and difficulty with waiting, as well as characteristics of inattentiveness or distractibility. These children find it difficult to discriminate among incoming stimuli – to screen out ambient sounds and to focus in on the relevant activity.

Organization Is Key

Even though parents and educators are cognizant that the actions of these children are unintentional, it is natural at times to become exhausted in our attempts to respond to the demands of the ADHD child. We tend to spend an inordinate amount of energy in responding to what seems to be their unquenchable energy or activity. However, rather than engaging in this relentless reactive "dance," we can take some proactive steps to design a framework for the ADHD child's life. The challenge is that this framework consists of an elaborate set of strategies, each of which requires planning and forethought. Checklists, schedules and behavioural management techniques must quickly become part of the daily routine.

A discussion of strategies for the ADHD child would not be complete without reference to pharmacological interventions. Naturally, there are inherent arguments surrounding the use of medication with young children; however, in some circumstances, the child must first be medicated in order to dampen or to dissipate the ADHD symptoms, and to permit the effective use of these intervention strategies.

Another critical element in the eventual success of these strategies is the need to engage in a candid discussion with the child about ADHD. The ADHD child is aware that something is impeding his/her progress in school, at home and in social relations, and it will probably be a relief when the issue is demystified. During these discussions, it is important to emphasize optimism. That is, that there are compensating strategies that can be learned through a development of self-awareness and self-monitoring techniques that will enable the child to function better in learning and social environments.

Generally speaking, the most important aspect to keep in mind when attempting to assist the ADHD child is the importance of "structure." ADHD children require clearly communicated routines and expectations. What this means is that there is a need to break down and structure the daily activities of the child. The second thing to keep in mind is that it is advisable to work through no more than one disruptive or unmanageable activity/behaviour at a time.

How It Works
A behaviour, usually chosen by both parents and child, is targeted for restructuring. This restructuring process requires the family to break down the activity or task into small chunks so that it can be monitored and tracked against a schedule or checklist. Then, if the behavioural expectation is met, a reward system must be in place to reinforce the desired behaviour. Any behaviour that is in need of improvement or restructuring must be explained to the child in simple, brief pieces and the desired behaviour must be modelled. The child must be reminded of what the desired behaviour looks like.

A necessary tool for the effective implementation of these strategies is either a flipchart, whiteboard or other device that can hold a place of prominence in your home; perhaps in the kitchen, or some other high traffic area. This whiteboard can be used to post important reminders or schedules that need to be followed. However, this does not mean that every routine must be placed on the board; remember that the ADHD child has a short attention span and only brief or small routines must be taught first and only one at a time. For example, if the problem is that the child doesn't remember to take a knapsack from the front hall to the bedroom and unload it after school, and, then in the morning does not remember to take the knapsack (including all the required school materials) to school, perhaps this routine can be set out on the whiteboard. Remember it is crucial that we don't overwhelm the child and that we ensure that the routine is SIMPLE.

For example, this routine could consist of four steps.

1) Take knapsack upstairs
2) Unload knapsack and bring down agenda for parents to check homework
3) Take knapsack downstairs in morning
4) Is notebook for class in knapsack? Writing utensil? Textbook?

(Naturally you would need to have the school schedule tacked near the whiteboard to ensure that required notebooks and texts were taken each day; also if child has not brought home agenda then back to school he/she goes.)

Once an activity or behaviour is completed to a satisfactory level (e.g. 80%), then the next important target behaviour or task can take prominence on the whiteboard and the previous accomplished task can be relegated to a notebook where all routinized procedures or tasks are held. This is not to say that the previous behaviour is ignored, but that a daily reminder of it must take place with a check mark if accomplished.

In order to maintain previous taught behaviours, what we refer to as behavioural management strategies, must be incorporated. In a nutshell, this requires tracking of behaviour. After an agreed upon level is accomplished, a reward is granted. The key behind maintaining the behaviour is either to offer a graduated level (smaller then larger) of rewards or preferred activity (money, food, praise, time on computer, whatever the child likes), change the rewards or extend your expectations. For example, if the target level for the knapsack activity is 8 out of 10 days then extend the time period for the reward to be granted to 9 out of 10 days. (Naturally, you must challenge the child to want to extend the time period or this strategy is counterproductive. We cannot go on rewarding a child forever; the ultimate goal is for self-management.)

Three Challenging Behaviours
There seems to be three challenging behaviours that both parent and educator alike agree to be in need of extinguishing or, if not possible, diminishing. They are described as follows:

1) Child completes only a portion of the independent task and is up doing something else.
An inevitable fact of ADHD is that the child cannot spend much time on a task. One reason for this is that the ADHD child expends a great amount of energy filtering out information whereas other people are able to do this quite easily. Accordingly, all distractions must be minimized in a setting where the ADHD is

required to focus. Studying should take place in a relatively sterile environment, devoid of as much stimuli as possible. Secondly, the ADHD child needs to take mental breaks, to be able to engage in some movement or activity. For example, 5-10 minute breaks can be provided at consistent intervals after about 30 minutes of homework.

A checklist or schedule can be set up to track the number of times the child is able to work on a task and then take a break at an agreed upon time (the break can consist of walking around, or whatever the child normally does when avoiding more work). In time we want the child to be cognizant of how long h/she can work on a task and when a break is needed. Ideally, we want the child to be able to manage his/her time without the use of a reward system.

A couple of points need to be made when discussing the area of homework. It is useful to teach your child how to prioritize tasks. You can teach your child to do the most important work first when he/she is able to focus. It is also useful to teach your child to focus on cues for important information in the material that is being read. The child can learn to focus on words such as "in summary…" or "the five reasons are…" Another useful strategy is to teach your child self-monitoring of his/her progress. A timer could be used every 10 minutes to keep on track and not leave things out. Children can also develop "To Do" lists to ensure that they keep track of their school work as well as housework. Any incentive for working too quickly must be removed and establishment of a time-to-complete a task is recommended.

Organizing materials and belongings seem to pose a challenge for ADHD children. You may want to establish specific places for belongings and incorporate checklists and rewards systems. Colour coding items that belong to certain routines or activities can also prove useful.

2) Child blurts out answers without waiting or cannot wait turn.

Another characteristic of ADHD is impulsivity. Here, it is important to establish wait times. For example, only after 10 minutes of working on a task, or after at least two attempts at working on the task may the child ask for help. Or if a child has a tendency to interrupt or call out, you can establish that the child can only have four "interruption" cards. When the cards are used no more interruptions are permitted or loss of a desirable activity takes place. Alternatively, you can offer wait time activities. While waiting, the child is to engage in one of a number of other activities as agreed upon by both you and the child.

3) Child cannot listen for long periods of time.

Two final characteristics of ADHD are a difficulty in listening and comprehending information. In an effort to obtain the child's attention it is imperative to visually and verbally cue the child. The verbal cues can take the form of using the child's name at the beginning of the direction or statement, or prior to giving instructions state in a directive, but supportive, fashion "Look at me." Visual cues include establishing eye contact or utilizing a colour card system (e.g. yellow card equals give me your attention). At the same time it is advisable to give the child opportunities to doodle, squeeze a ball or tap a pencil on the thigh while listening as this permits them to be actively involved.

ADHD children have difficulty with auditory short-term memory thus it is important to give an overview of what you are about to say. Link the information to prior knowledge; check for understanding and ask the child to summarize or repeat the information; provide information in small chunks and highlight important information on a piece of paper. Also, let the child know when a task will be finished and the focus must be changed (for example, "in two minutes it will be time for dinner") and, finally, keep a schedule of activities on the whiteboard for the child to remember.

I hope that these strategies provide some direction for you and your families when responding to the needs of the ADHD child. While a lot of time must be spent on organizing and developing schedules, in the long run it is the only method that is outlined in the literature to be effective.

This article originally appeared in the SNAP newsmagazine, Vol. 18#2, March/April 2002. © 2002 Society of Special Needs Adoptive Parents

Dr. Julie Conry Highlights a Multidimensional Approach to ADHD
by Sara Graefe

I decided to hunt down some perspectives on ADHD from a local expert. I spoke with psychologist Dr. Julie Conry, SNAP Board member and specialist in child behaviour and development, in her office at UBC's Department of Educational Psychology and Special Education.

Addressing the Underlying Causes
SNAP: *Could you give us a bit of background on your work and interest in ADD? Like many of us at SNAP, I have a tendency to think of you first in terms of your work with Fetal Alcohol Syndrome.*

DR. C: My work with FAS came later. Attention Deficit Hyperactivity was the area which first sparked my interest in other neurologically-based problems. Back in 1982, I had the opportunity to do an internship with a neuropsychiatrist in southern California by the name of Sydney Walker III. He had written an article in *Psychology Today* called "The Drugging of the North American Child," and it was at that point, which was actually in the mid-seventies, where Ritalin was being used a great deal, and there was an out-and-out controversy over whether children should be medicated and what the eventual outcomes would be.

In that particular article, he talked about all of the medical bases for Attention Deficit Hyperactivity. What he was finding with all the children that came to him—and they were coming from all over the United States--was that in something like over 90% of the cases of children with Attention Deficit Hyperactivity, he was able to identify a medical cause for that disorder, and a *treatable* medical cause. It is sort of akin to the idea that if you have a headache, you can treat the headache with Tylenol or painkillers—but isn't it important to know whether that headache is caused by stress, or because you have the flu, or because you have a brain tumour? It is the *underlying cause* that's important. You can sometimes mask the symptoms, but you may be neglecting that underlying cause. Dr. Walker was trying to put forth the idea that you really should be looking for the underlying cause *first* before you attempt to simply mask the symptoms.

At that point, I became very interested in the medical bases for a lot of children's learning and behavioural problems. At that point—which is now only twelve to fifteen years ago—that was not widely understood, whereas today, parents and teachers are very much more aware of the medical conditions that can then relate to learning and behaviour problems. So I think that's been a major shift in this period of time.

SNAP: *It's exciting that you got to work with Dr. Walker and take part in the beginnings of this movement.*

DR. C: What was important for me was that this was the final piece in the puzzle. There was always a piece missing in doing assessments and trying to figure out children's learning and behavioural problems, and so when I began to realize that sometimes there are these medical bases that had not been treated or identified, that became the missing link. It began to explain a lot of problems that didn't have explanations before. Then, what I learned from Sydney Walker III was an approach—that Attention Deficit Hyperactivity was really a *collection* of symptoms that had a whole *range* of underlying causes. The tendency to put a diagnosis of ADHD gives a name to this collection of behaviours, but it doesn't necessarily address the underlying cause, and maybe that's what we should be doing. When the label ADD is applied, usually it means a treatment, which is stimulant medication—which in most cases is Ritalin, although other medications are used as well.

Remove the Poison First

SNAP: *The use of Ritalin has been hotly debated for years. After a child's diagnosis, parents are often left asking, "Now what?" Is it worth considering alternatives to medication?*

DR. C: Again, if we're looking at ADD as a *symptom* of an underlying cause, then there are a whole range of underlying causes. For example, one of those associated causes is Fetal Alcohol Syndrome, and the brain damage that, as we know, occurs because of prenatal alcohol exposure. That's one certain kind of situation where maybe the Ritalin is helpful—sometimes it is, sometimes it isn't.

As another example, children who have been exposed to lead often exhibit distractibility and hyperactivity, and so there has been a lot of interest recently in the fact that children can be exposed to lead through automobile exhaust, although less so now with unleaded gas, but certainly in older homes where there are lead pipes and old paints on the walls that are chipping off. And it doesn't take very much for a child to become poisoned by lead through exposure. A few years ago, it was discovered within our schools that children were being exposed to lead through the drinking fountains, and so it became established procedure that in the morning, the janitors would run the water in the taps for ten minutes before the children arrived at school in order to flush out the accumulation of lead that would have contaminated the water. This is now less of a problem, but children can still have that as a cause.

There can be other medical causes, such as hyperthyroidism, and other metabolic causes, so if you can treat *those* causes, there's no need to use Ritalin. Let's remove the poison from the child—I think that's really what needs to be done first, and the concern has been that maybe children have been prescribed Ritalin without all these other medical workouts being done prior to that. Of course, children who are extremely hyperactive are very difficult to manage. Parents are often at their wits' ends; they want a quick fix, and we sort of hope that a pill is going do it. Well, a pill alone is usually *not* going to do it, although it can make some very dramatic changes in children's behaviour.

I have to say that ten years ago, I was really opposed to the use of Ritalin with children, but now I have seen families that would not be together today were it not for the fact that Ritalin has been used and has worked very effectively with their children. I just get concerned in some instances where it isn't monitored very closely, so that if the Ritalin doesn't work, the parents are simply told, *"well, give him more,"* and if that doesn't work, *"give him more, give him more, give him more"*—and then pretty soon, we have an overly-sedated child, rather than one whose abilities are functional because of normalizing what is a neurotransmitter problem. Look into the underlying causes first, and then medication is often a good option.

Today we really believe that it shouldn't be *just* the medication, but usually it should be the medication *in combination* with other behavioural techniques where the child is learning to take some control of his/her behaviour with the help of the medication.

SNAP: *What about foods? There seem to be mixed opinions about the influence of diet on ADHD.*

DR. C: Again, it's one of many possible causes. I've had personal experience working with an allergist/nutritionist, where we studied children with Attention Deficit Hyperactivity, and for some children, modifications in the diet were highly effective. I think any kind of treatment where we say, *"this is the treatment for ADD"*, we're going to be wrong, because that's assuming that ADD children are a homogenous group. When you begin to recognize that there are so many different underlying causes, then of course one treatment isn't going to work for all children. And so again, we've been hoping for one thing that's going to be effective for all these children, and that's unreal.

Parenting

SNAP: *So much of the literature on ADD is geared towards the classroom. Do you have any advice for parents?*

DR. C: I think in fact there are quite a few books now that talk about parenting a child with ADD. There's certainly a lot more available than there has been in the past. The same principles apply, whether it's the child at home or the child at school—rules have to be very clear, and you have to try to be extremely consistent and reinforce the behaviour immediately. This may be much harder to deal with at home because there are so many things to do in a day. The impact of a child who has attention deficit hyperactivity on the other family members or other children is significant because ADHD children can be *so* disruptive. Sometimes children who have ADD are also quite aggressive, or very hyperactive and also extremely impulsive. Those children require nearly constant supervision, because things go wrong with them all day long, and it's very difficult to manage at home. But the same things apply, whether it's at home or at school.

SNAP: *What do you recommend for parents who suspect their child has ADD?*

DR. C: One of the things that we try to do in an assessment is see how pervasive the condition is—do we see it occurring in more than one setting? I think this is the caution with the diagnosis of ADD—is this something that we only see at school and we really don't see in other places? Do we just see it at home, but not at school? And of course, you never see it in the doctor's office, because when you go to see the doctor, this is a novel situation and all of a sudden the child is able to control this attention deficit hyperactivity—and so the doctor says, *"Well, I don't see anything wrong here."* It's something we want to observe in more than one setting, and from more than one perspective.

I really think that if the parents are looking at this demon and are saying, *"I wonder if this is ADD,"* it probably is. It's at least ADD *symptoms*. Perhaps the cause is something as simple as time to enforce the child's bedtime and routines—maybe it is a situation where there are parenting differences that can change a child's behaviour. Or is it something that has another medical cause? That's what the medical doctor needs to sort out. I think when you see the symptoms, the first thing is to collect information to describe the condition—where do we see it, how extreme is it—and to take that information to the doctor to say, *"OK, this is what we're seeing—what are we dealing with?"* Then look for those other medical causes, as well as the environmental causes.

Growing Up

SNAP: *What about the transition into adulthood? There seems to be growing awareness of adults who have ADD.*

DR. C: I think we then have to consider *what is ADD associated with?* For example, something around 25% of children with ADD also have learning disabilities. A certain number of them might also have conduct disorders or demonstrate aggression, and so on. It's often those other complicating factors that are going to influence their transition to adulthood.

But having said that—for many individuals, once they reach adolescence some of the symptoms of hyperactivity subside, but often the attention deficit remains. Just being easily distracted, whether it's working on a job, or needing to move around, means that there are some occupations that are going to be very good for a person who has ADD, and others that are not. For example, one young woman was very successful because her job was house cleaning. She cleaned houses like a tornado, and then she went home and cleaned her own. That was wonderful for her, because she was constantly moving. Another young man did really well because he worked in a warehouse where he had to go racing back and forwards, climbing up ladders, picking up auto parts, organizing them for customers, and so on—again, it was perfect for him. But another individual who has a desk job may be extremely frustrated. It's really important to try to match the job with the characteristics of the individual.

It is true for many individuals with ADD that one part of it can be poor social skills. Again, this can relate to the impulsivity, or a broader learning disability, which is the inability to perceive social cues. Very often, children with ADD are seen as immature—they are difficult to have on teams because they can't wait their turn or follow the rules, and they get mad and walk away in the middle of the game, and so on. The social skills deficits that sometimes accompany ADD often continue and cause difficulties as people approach adulthood, so often having satisfactory relationships becomes a problem.

Now, there are many adults who hear about ADD and say, "Oh, I wonder if *that's* what the problem was when I was younger *and* now." To put a name to it— *this is what it is*—is extremely helpful, for both children and adults. It's a huge relief—*oh, that's the reason for it.* For children who have had ADD, going through school often has been such a struggle, and it isn't because they're not smart, but because of this other problem.

Attention Deficit Is Real

SNAP: *What about the current backlash? Some professionals are claiming that ADD is just a label, and doesn't really exist.*

DR. C: My response to that is—I think a few families would be happy to loan their child to them for a weekend, and *then* they'll believe it.

It *is* a real condition. There's no question about it. The difficulty comes in that it is a continuum—it isn't as though you have measles or you don't have measles. The definition includes the fact that the problems of the hyperactivity or distractibility or impulsivity are extreme enough that they significantly impact day-to-day functioning, whether it's at school or at home or on a job. Again, there is certainly a tolerance level of parents or teachers, and a personality match where some teachers are better able to manage an ADD child than others. But at the same time, on an objective basis—and we have some computerized measurements—we can say, this child is *not* able to attend. So we have both the subjective measures, where individuals might disagree as to how severe this problem really is, but we also have computerized objective measures that show us that this child, under the most optimum conditions, is not able to sustain his attention. There's no question about it—it's obviously a very real condition.

ADHD can be over-diagnosed, and everybody would have an experience where a child might be called ADD when that really isn't the case. I think people *do* need an explanation for their child's difficulties, whatever it is—and so when they hear about something or read about something, they may say, *"oh, that's my child."* In terms of reported estimates—are we talking about a condition that occurs 3% of the time? There are estimates all the way up to 20% of the time, and some people start saying, *"well, it must not exist at all."* Because it doesn't make sense that it could occur 20% of the time. That's what people are reacting to, as opposed to the condition existing or not existing.

Maybe we *do* have more children now who have ADD. And maybe we have more children because there are things like Fetal Alcohol Syndrome and drug exposure that are associated with, or have as part of their symptoms, ADD. And perhaps there are some more influences—maybe we are talking about pesticide exposure, out in the valley where the farms are—we know that that's another toxic influence for some children. Maybe it's the pollution. Maybe it's some of these other things. Perhaps we are seeing more ADD now. People *are* noticing it more.

CAUSES OF ATTENTION DEFICIT DISORDER

Medical
- Hyperthyroidism
- Sleep apnea syndrome
- Pinworms
- Intercurrent illness

Neurologic
- Prematurity
- Congenital infection
- Difficult delivery
- Perinatal asphyxia
- Head trauma
- Encephalitis (particularly from Herpes simplex)
- Sydenham chorea
- Temporal lobe epilepsy

Toxic
- Phenobarbital
- Antihistamines
- Lead
- Phenothiazines
- Alcohol in utero
- Food substances

Psychologic
- Anxiety
- Depression
- Manic syndrome

Social-Environmental
- Overstimulation
- Boredom
- Failure of limit-setting
- (?) Fluorescent lighting

Genetic-Constitutional
- Familial pattern
- Temperament

Developmental
- Relatively slower CNS maturation in males

(Reference: Herskowitz, J & Rosman, N.P. *Pediatrics, Neurology and Psychiatry - Common Ground.* Toronto: Collier Macmillan Canada, Inc. 1982.)

This article originally appeared in the SNAP newsletter, Vol. 12 #1, spring 1996. © 1996 Society of Special Needs Adoptive Parents

Creating a Positive Environment for Everyone

by Beryl Trimble

It is important, when considering ADD/ADHD and the family, that any day-to-day living strategies are created to include the whole family, and not just the individual who has the diagnosis of ADD/ADHD. Most commonly, strategies are focused on the individual, and create some sort of management program for that individual. However, it is critical that the family is seen, and sees itself, as a unit, all working towards creating the positive environment that encompasses the lives of all members.

How each member interacts with each other, including the individual with ADD/ADHD, can give a clear picture of the projected success of any family management program. Family management and not individual management is the focus that is necessary in creating a positive living environment. The following tips may be helpful to families striving to make sense of life with ADD/ADHD, and who want to bring some control into their day-to-day living.

1. Appropriate treatment for ADD/ADHD can only begin once an accurate diagnosis of ADD/ADHD has been made. Although this might seem obvious, it is not always.

2. Education for all members of the family. Everyone needs to learn the facts about ADD/ADHD, as this is the first step in the treatment. When everyone understands what is happening, many issues will be resolved immediately. Each member will have different questions and it is important that every effort is made to answer all questions.

3. It is well known that people can be set up for failure and this can well happen within the family situation. When speaking about the individual with ADD/ADHD, all family members should focus on the positive attributes, rather than identify negative issues. This includes talking within extended family units, as well as out in the community. It may be difficult for some members of a family to live with the direct outbursts of the member with ADD/ADHD, but with humour and honesty, this can become a very positive part of any social interaction. It is important that all family members are able to discuss their feelings within the family unit, when problems arise.

4. Treatment can be sabotaged if family members believe that ADD/ADHD is an excuse for bad behaviour or that it is caused by laziness. It is very important that everyone understand that ADD/ADHD is no one's fault. No one is to blame, not the parents, siblings, extended family or the person with ADD/ADHD. Honest, open discussion is critical around this point to prevent lingering feelings. Everyone

in the family is involved in the day-to-day, which means they should also be involved in the resolving of problems together, and in the treatment of the individual. Make sure that extended family members are aware of the ADD/ADHD diagnosis. There may be things that they know about ADD/ADHD and some other member may have it, even if it is undiagnosed. This disclosure can be very reassuring and comforting for everyone.

5. Each family member should have the attention that they need, or at least there should be some balance. Often when one member has a diagnosis of ADD/ADHD, the siblings get less attention, and the focus of all social interaction is directed at the individual with ADD/ADHD. All members should be able to talk through their concerns, frustrations and anger, all of which are normal reactions in any household, but resolution of which is critical in the treatment of a person with ADD/ADHD. Issues that are pushed to one side, without resolution or discussion, will resurface later as a power struggle, resentment or detachment. At this point treatment cannot be successful. Continued negotiation between all family members is critically important. Make sure that problem areas are defined; like bedtime, mealtimes, transition times, and that all family members are consulted with regard to resolution and suggestions.

6. Family negotiations can break down. Outside support is crucial at these times. A professional therapist can be very helpful in calming things down. It could well be helpful to have videotaped family role play at these times, so that each member can see himself or herself behave. People with ADD/ADHD often are poor self-observers, and may well be unaware of their behaviour, rather than being unwilling to change. Seeing things in a different way can be very positive for all members of the family.

7. Try to turn negative issues into positive ones. Laugh a lot and encourage family members to see positive goals. It is hard for a family living with ADD/ADHD to remain positive, but the future can be amazing if this is done. Families should strive to stay away from getting embroiled in power struggles, or escalating arguments. Members should try to walk away rather than get involved in struggles.

8. Family members should each know what the rules are and how they apply to them. They should be aware of their responsibilities and the consequences of breaking rules. These rules should be agreed on before anger and resentment set in. They should be agreed on right at the outset of treatment.

9. It is well known that children with ADD/ADHD can be delightful one day and disruptive and turbulent the next. This makes it difficult for a parent or caregiver to be consistent in what they feel. It is best for the family balance if the parent and other members of the family can strive to find some middle road. This way the fluctuations are less erratic. The parent needs to preserve stability in the family

unit, even though this can be very difficult at times. Being consistent is important in the treatment of ADD/ADHD, and a united front between parents is crucial.

10. Take notice of all information you receive from outside sources, therapists, teachers, pediatrician, support groups, family, friends and others. Often family members will listen to what they hear from someone outside of the family. Families should not be ashamed to use whatever supports are out there for them. Cultivate as many supports as possible. It does not show failure in any way to reach out for help, but it does show that the family is interested in doing the very best they can to achieve success in the treatment of ADD/ADHD and happiness for the whole family. Support groups are a great way to find out that your family is not the only one dealing with the stresses of living with ADD/ADHD.

11. Family members need to realize that, apart from being members of the family unit, they have to be able to function independently outside of the family. It is easy to become so focused with family issues that independence gets lost along the way and family control becomes excessive within the unit. Everyone needs to see themselves independently of the family. This is critical for keeping the stress levels down on a day-to-day basis.

12. Treatment for ADD/ADHD can seem to be ineffective for a long time, and it is easy to get discouraged. Don't give up. Hope is what keeps everyone going and, in those moments when it seems as though things couldn't get worse, remember that things will soon be better. Tell yourself that kids grow up fast and many adults with ADD/ADHD live full, productive, energetic, creative and independent lives. And they make honest and intuitive friends and partners.

Never underestimate the power of the family. It is important that this power be used for positive healing, not for criticism and inflicting pain. Healing within the family can be more effective and rapid than any medications or therapies, and the strength of the family cannot be overstressed. A family that is willing to work in a positive manner with all its members can see the most amazing results in the treatment of ADD/ADHD. The family unit should be supported in every way possible, in order for it to implement and continue such critically important work.

This article originally appeared in the SNAP newsmagazine, Vol. 18#2, March/April 2002. © 2002 Society of Special Needs Adoptive Parents

ADHD & Youth:

Social Difficulties

by Lorelei Faulkner

Over half of children with ADHD have difficulties in adolescence and, later, adulthood. The symptoms of ADHD affect youth in a variety of ways. The typical "hyperactivity" seen in younger children often becomes internalized in youth with a feeling of restlessness, needing to be on the go or feeling "bored." Maturity is often delayed, with youth functioning about 2-3 years below their chronological age. They can be more explosive and reactive as they move through puberty than non-ADHD youth. Peer pressure and increased expectations both academically and at home can lead to demoralization if the youth is not successful in these areas.

Youth with ADHD are often drawn to high-energy sports. This can be a great outlet for much of their energy and can lead to areas of success. However, impulsivity and hyperactivity can lead to accidents. Safety discussions are important to ensure the youth understands what to do should a problem arise. Parents often feel worried about their children and this can make it difficult for families to handle the challenges they face. Some youth have had continuing problems with gross motor skills and may need accommodation within their physical education curriculum.

Immaturity seen in many youth with ADHD can have a dramatic impact on their social relationships with peers. Adolescence is the time of individuation and increased relations with peers. It can be difficult for the parent to allow independence when so often it has resulted in trouble for their ADHD child.

Parents and teachers expect a certain level of maturity as a child moves into adolescence and this is often delayed in youth with ADHD. One area of particular difficulty is safe driving. This needs to be considered when your 16 year old with ADHD, who is impulsive, inattentive, distractible and emotionally functioning at a 13 year old level, wants to get a driver's license. Structured expectations need to be put in place, such as enrolling the youth in driver's education, encouraging him or her to obtain part time work to help with costs, ensuring follow-through of expectations in the home, or extending the time period that the youth must drive with the parent as a passenger.

Problems with academic achievement do not go away in adolescence and many youth need remedial support to help with gaps in learning, co-existing learning disabilities and general organization and planning. Peer or adult tutors can be helpful and may minimize arguing between parent and youth. Having the youth participate in a portion of school team meetings helps prepare for self-advocacy later on. This process can start in elementary school, even if the child is only involved for a short period of time.

Many youth with ADHD are happy and healthy, with few ups and downs. However there are some youth who constantly struggle with the world around them. Some youth with ADHD become socially isolated or gravitate towards a less desirable peer group. With low self-esteem and demoralization, youth can become depressed and suicidal. Others who have positive self esteem and an activity in which they excel usually do much better even if school is not their strong suit.

Youth with ADHD can be impulsive in their social interactions and often make poor choices in attempts to make friends. Usually the behaviour is embarrassing although sometimes the youth can get into serious trouble with adults or the law in these situations. Some youth will be sexually impulsive. For example, boys may behave in a silly manner such as exposing or mooning to get attention. Girls may find themselves in situations that are dangerous when they have not stopped to think of the consequences of their behaviour. They may not feel they have the power to stop and say no. Helping the youth to think through potential problems before they occur helps to give some skills to manage these situations.

Some youth with ADHD may "self-medicate," the drug of choice often being cannabis. Many parents feel this is not so bad; however, long term use of cannabis can create more problems for a youth with inattention, poor impulse control and procrastination. Research shows that youth with ADHD who have been adequately medically treated are less likely to engage in drugs and alcohol than youth who are not treated effectively. Addictions can be a major problem with youth and adults with ADHD due to poor impulse control. This is not limited to drugs, but can include gambling and internet activity.

As a parent what can you do? Ensure a medical professional who understands ADHD has adequately assessed your youth. Keep the lines of communication open between you, your youth and the professionals you work with. Ensure academic assessments have been done to determine if a learning disability is a factor and if accommodations need to be made and documented. Maintain activities of success. Negotiate the rules and expectations in the home. Plan a meeting when you and your youth have time. Turn off the TV. Brainstorm and listen; no idea is a bad idea. Put the consensus in writing and make a date for a review of the outcome. Positively acknowledge when your youth has been compliant. Try not to overreact when rules are broken. Try very hard not to argue or become provoked in discussions with your youth. It is okay for them to have the last word.

Self-esteem is very important in the success of every individual, regardless of limitations. Allow your youth to participate in decision making about care, school and activities. Set realistic expectations for your youth and yourselves as parents. Many parents are concerned that their youth may be manipulating them. Positive reinforcement of expected behaviour is the best route. Long term consequences or grounding is not effective. Structure versus control works best for youth with ADHD. Make use of the resources in your school and community, such as counsellors, psychologists, sports leaders, religious groups and activity leaders.

Remember:
Responsibility + Compliance = Freedom
Look for the POSITIVE!
Ignore negative behaviors, unless life threatening.
Special activities or talents or part-time work = Positive Self Esteem

This article originally appeared in the SNAP newsmagazine, Vol. 18#2, March/April 2002. © 2002 Society of Special Needs Adoptive Parents

Striving for Positive Change:
An Adoptive Parent's Perspective
by Donna McCreesh

As the parents of five children ages 9-32, we closely resemble the Brady Bunch (yours, ours and adopted). We first experienced ADHD with child number four. To me he had always been a highly spirited and busy boy, as well as strong willed. We read the parenting books, did the diet, set up the rules and organizational charts, provided motivators and incentives, kept him busy with sports and outdoor activities, and worked closely with the school. He had done his best to stay on task and meet the mark. He was an A student. He spent most mornings in the hall due to his behaviour and then would go off to enrichment classes, which to him seemed to be a reward. To us this made no sense. It wasn't until age 13, when his world began to fall apart, that he was actually diagnosed with ADHD and a learning disability.

We found one staff member at the school who believed in our son and would work with us. We sought medical and psychological help to diagnose the problem. We kept a journal to record observations especially if any medications were being introduced. We learned everything we could about ADHD and the disability.

Our son had to learn good study habits, how to be organized, and how he learned best for him. We altered the presentation of information by trying taped classes and having textbooks on tape. Written materials were enlarged and spaced more. A scribe recorded his exams.

We advocated for our son every chance we had. We set him up so he could succeed. He knew that we loved him, that we believed in him, and that we were there for him. We listened to him as he vented and, with support, he rose to the challenges ahead. He graduated and went on to university. He still loves and needs his sports, but don't ride a car with him! Little did we know that all this was merely preparation for child number five.....our next adventure called Brendan.

Brendan came to us as a premature infant from a possibly high risk background. We had monthly home visits from the IDP (Infant Development Program) nurse beginning at three months old. His development was quite different right from birth, but we kept hoping that by the magic age of two years old, he would suddenly be like other infants in his play group.   He was a 24-hour-per-day job. I had to hold his wrist in order to get my teeth brushed, otherwise he would be out the door, and I don't mean the bathroom door. Soon he was diagnosed by a team of professionals as having autism with severe ADHD. He didn't eat, didn't sleep and practically never stopped running. He was our little Duracell bunny!

He is now nine years old and attends school full-time. What we learned through our parenting experience was that it's important to learn everything you can about the disorder. We learned to use simple language and to express our demands in a positive way. We told him what we wanted him to do versus what not to do. We implemented calming activities such as wrapping him in a warm blanket and rocking him. We made a "safe place" for him to go when things got rough. We also worked very closely with a behaviour consultant to identify behaviours, their precursors and antecedent events.

We worked to build on his strengths and to use reinforcers as motivators. We developed a structured and predictable setting for him. We developed cues and prompts to get his attention such as hand clapping. As a parent of two children who have ADHD, I feel that these are the best strategies to use. Stay calm even though he's standing in the middle of the Trans-Canada Highway. Stay calm!! Never enter into a power struggle as you will always lose. ADHD kids are often great debaters and would make wonderful lawyers. Don't take things personally. Although he may be freaking out at you, chances are it might be that he can't find a sock or he left his homework at school. It's usually nothing to do with you. Acknowledge the emotion in this case and attempt to look beyond it. Very important: always keep a sense of humour! Choose your battles as there will be lots of them. Choose the important ones and let the others go. Patience is a good thing. Allow plenty of time for transitions. The more these kids hurry the worse it gets so stay calm and be patient. Just remember that the child is doing his or her best and will get there eventually.

Here's a little something to remember about rules: write your house rules on a board or make a visual display. No yelling, just point to it and ask what is the rule. This way it's about the rules and not about you or the child. I find that it's a good thing to allow for natural consequences, that is, unless it puts someone in danger.

Set up routines; for instance, let them know what's expected of them for morning and evening care, and at mealtimes. I find it's very helpful to structure both the child's environment and activities. Allow the child to make his or her own choices; don't ask "Do you need a coat?" but rather, "Would you like your red coat or your blue one?" Remember that any activity is only as good as your enthusiasm and presentation. Brendan's birth announcement read: "His little smile makes it all worthwhile." It still helps me to remember this today.

This article originally appeared in the SNAP newsmagazine, Vol. 18#2, March/April 2002. © 2002 Society of Special Needs Adoptive Parents

conduct disorder

AGGRESSIVE AND DISRUPTIVE
BEHAVIOUR IS ONE OF THE
MORE ENDURING
DYSFUNCTIONS OF CHILDREN.
– Arthur M. Horne
Thomas V. Sayger

Towards a Definition of Conduct Disorder

by Lisa Marie Gruger

Conduct disordered youth are known by many names. Horne and Sayger (1990) have suggested the following labels to describe individuals with conduct disorder, as they appear in varying environments: in the medical field they are the hyperactive, hyper kinetic child, in correctional services they are the delinquent or young offender, in social services they are known as a social deviant, antisocial child, or victim of abuse; and, in the education system, they are often labelled a discipline or management problem, and emotionally handicapped youth, or a behaviour disordered student (p.8).

While a number of formal definitions and subsequent diagnostic criteria exist for the condition, despite the considerable work that has been done in terms of understanding the profile of the conduct disordered individual, there remains a lack of clarity in the field regarding specifically "who" is the conduct disordered child. Indeed, it is well recognized that the conduct disorder is neither a well-defined nor a homogeneous construct and that there remains much confusion about the terminology and categories used to describe the same cluster of behaviours (Dodge, 1990; Gardener, 1992). Dodge (1990) in fact argues that conduct disorder is a diagnosis often made by default and maintains that the term conduct disorder is at best "a heuristic term to describe heterogeneous phenomenon with differing etiologies and causes" (p. 699).

While perhaps this fact confounds the process of seeking an accurate diagnosis of the condition, and thus complicates the task of both assessing and planning for treatment programs, it is, nevertheless, a critical point to acknowledge and to integrate into one's understanding of conduct disorder. This disagreement, in itself, points to one of the key characteristics of the disorder and is perhaps the most important thing to keep in mind when working with such individuals: conduct disorders constitute a complex and heterogeneous set of antisocial behaviours and therefore the term belies "remarkably broad and diverse patterns of functioning... which can vary markedly in severity, chronicity and frequency" and which can manifest themselves in a variety of combinations (Kazdin, 1993, p. 277). Recognition of this fact will place the professional, whose task it is to assess and develop an appropriate treatment plan for individuals with conduct disorder, at a solidly realistic, albeit challenging, starting point.

While a definition and subsequent diagnosis of this condition remains controversial in North American literature, a uniform diagnosis of conduct disorder has evolved with a consistent or compatible set of characteristics that are understood as such. In its broadest sense, a conduct disorder is commonly agreed to constitute externalizing or "acting out" problems which refer to a constellation of behaviours characterized by noncompliance, aggression, destruction, attention problems, impulsivity, hyperactivity and "delinquent" types of behaviour (McMahon, 1994). The connecting thread in the array of behaviours that make up this disorder is the violation of social norms and basic rights of others (Davison and Neale, 1990). A conduct disorder is frequently evidenced by a significant impairment in everyday functioning, be it at home or at school, or when the child's behaviours are regarded as unmanageable by significant others (Kazding, 1987).

What separates conduct disordered behaviour from normal behaviour problems of aggression and defiance, which research suggests have relatively high prevalence at specific ages of development (i.e. defiance at age two or lying at age six), is that the child or adolescent with conduct disorder experiences problems that are "persistent and extreme patterns... which reflect a serious clinical problem with broad personal and social impact" (Toth, 1990, p.9). That is, the conduct disordered child does not "outgrow" these antisocial behaviours (Toth, 1990). Rather, they are increasingly brought to the attention of professionals in many fields because of their frequency, intensity, repetitiveness and chronicity.

This is the starting point. However, before considering the formal diagnostic criteria most commonly used, this author contends that there are several complicating issues that the careful practitioner must keep in mind. Already mentioned is the fact that conduct disorders are heterogeneous and that different agencies know them by different names and in their different manifestations as dictated by setting and by application of differing criteria. Further, there has been increasing recognition of specific issues surrounding the confounding factors of differing developmental courses and degrees of conduct disorder, gender, and comorbidity and their relation to a formal criteria. It is critical that the implications of each of these issues be carefully considered when assessing and/or acknowledging a diagnosis of conduct disorder; and more importantly, when considering treatment for these individuals.

Prevalence

Schlebusch made the statement in 1979 that "it would be difficult for any student of the problem to arbitrarily answer the question of exactly how prevalent conduct disorders are at any given period due to various difficulties, both practical and theoretical" (p.25). The overlap of this condition with other conditions and confounding issues such as gender, age, stage of development and potentially differing etiologies and subtypes, further complicates the issue. Nevertheless, there appears to be a general consensus in the literature to indicate that conduct disorders make up one of the most significant types of psychological disorder in children (Davison & Neale, 1990; Kazdin, 1987). Schelbusch (1979) suggests that although statistics vary considerably and we do not yet have a reliable index of the incidence of psychopathology in adolescence, we can get some idea from a few selected studies.

In a review of the current literature, Kazdin (1993) assessed that, conservatively, estimates in prevalence range from 2 to 6%. Shamsie (1990) points to findings of a study based in Ontario that suggests the rate to be 5.5% The DSM IV (1994) suggests that the incidence of conduct disorder appears to have increased over the last decade and may now be as high as 6 to 16% in males under 18 and 2 to 9% for females. An interesting point raised by Phelps and McClintock (1994) suggests that there may be differing prevalence rates not only for different genders, but also for different subtypes, with moderate cases representing 12% and severe cases representing 4%. Further, Kazding (1987) found that rates are significantly elevated for specific ages and behaviour when youths report on their activities. For example, he found that 50% of youth between 13 and 18 admit to theft, 35% to assault, 45% to property destruction, and 60% to aggressiveness, drug abuse, vandalism and arson (p.16).

Another measure for the prevalence of conduct disorder is the extent to which referrals to clinical services include antisocial behaviour. Estimates have indicated that referrals to outpatient clinics for aggressiveness, conduct problems and antisocial behaviours encompass from one-third to one-half of child and adolescent cases (Kazdin, 1987; Horne & Sayger, 1990; Shamsie, 1990) and Mash & Barkley (1989) suggest that 33 to 75% of clinic referrals consist of individuals with conduct disorder. Still, as estimates are typically based primarily on referral rates they may be somewhat on the low side if one considers that a large number of children, particularly girls, with this condition may never formally be referred for mental health services (Phelps & McClintock, 1994).

Gender Issues

Robins (1991) points out that one of the most stable of all observations in the literature on conduct disorder is the "high rate of conduct disorder in boys as compared to girls" and that "why this occurs, to what extent it is biological and to what extent it is a culturally determined factor is yet to be settled" (p.204). Zahn-Waxler(1993) echoes a similar concern indicating that "we are still some distance from answers regarding the etiology of conduct disorder in males and females, linkages between theories, empirical data and diagnostic outcomes" (p.84). But while we may not yet have all the answers, what is most important is that the questions are being raised and that these questions flag yet another significant consideration for those who work with conduct disordered children and youth.

A common estimate of the comparative prevalence of conduct disorder in boys versus girls is typically reported to be 9% in boys under age 18 and 2% in girls (Toth,1991). Schwartz(1989) suggests that the likelihood for boys to develop conduct disorders is four to eight times greater than for girls; whereas, Kazdin (1987) reports that conduct disorders are at least three times more common among boys and that sex differences further affect the age of onset. Girls tend to engage in conduct disordered behaviour starting between ages 14 and 16; whereas, for boys, many have become engaged in antisocial behaviour before the age of 11.

These differences have been linked to research on early and late starter models of conduct disorder, and the suggestion is made that conduct disorder may have a different developmental course in females. McMahon (1994) and Hinshaw, Lahey and Hart (1993) point out that components of the early-onset pathway for boys have failed to find similar support in girls and that girls may be more likely to enter the late starter pathway. In support of this, the DSM IV (1994) also makes a vague reference to the fact that "childhood onset type is much more common in males," implying that for girls, adolescent onset may be more common (p.86). But are males somehow more predisposed to an earlier and more severe form of conduct disorder than are females? McMahon (1994) suggests that of the few studies that have examined developmental causes of conduct disorder in girls, contradictory findings have been reported concerning whether there is a differential prognosis for boys and girls with respect to later display of conduct disorder. Walker, Colvin and Ramsey (1995) along with Zahn-Waxler (1993) make the argument that, despite gender differences, there is "considerable overlap between males and females on problems of conduct" (p.81). In order that this female population of conduct disordered girls is no longer ignored or sidestepped in issues surrounding classification, assessment and intervention, it is imperative that prospective care givers attempt to understand why these girls have not been recognized in the past. Several reasons for the vague understanding of female conduct disorder have been proposed.

The Issue of Comorbidity

The effort to define conduct disorder is further complicated by mounting evidence in recent research that, while in itself it constitutes a cluster of behavioural problems and can be seen as a syndrome, this disorder is most often not found in isolation. Indeed, there has been a plethora of studies in the past five years that focus on and which indicate that there is considerable overlap of conduct disorder with other conditions. More specifically, conduct disorders have been found to coexist with the two other major types of externalizing behaviour: oppositional defiant disorder and attention deficit/hyperactivity, along with anxiety and depression, substance abuse and learning problems (Forness, Kavalc, King and Kasari, 1994). In addition to these comorbid conditions, Fetal Alcohol Syndrome, Fragile X syndrome and traumatic brain injury are recognized to produce symptoms of conduct disorder and thus might also be seen as types of co-occurring conditions.

This article is excerpted from a full-length paper, written as part of Lisa Marie Gruger's graduate work in Clinical Psychology, and originally appeared in the SNAP newsletter, Vol. 14 #1, spring 1998. It is reprinted here with permission of the author.

Conduct Disorder from an Attachment Perspective:

Dr. Moretti Discusses Implications for Parenting

by Sara Graefe

Conduct disorder is often considered an untreatable condition that is best dealt with through the criminal justice system. This attitude is reflected in the public outcry for "get tough" approaches for young offenders and the implementation of boot camps in some jurisdictions. While there is no proven short-term, simple cure for conduct disorder, a growing body of research shows that getting tough is rarely effective in reducing antisocial behaviour—and that other alternatives do exist.

Multi-modal, family and community-oriented interventions have proven to be valuable. These approaches typically address the child's functioning in all areas of their day-to-day lives. They also take into account the fact that conduct disorder can have a range of underlying causes, and is often accompanied by other conditions requiring intervention such as attention deficit disorder, fetal alcohol syndrome, depression and substance abuse. Certain programs, such as the Response Program here in British Columbia, are based on attachment theory, as recent research supports a link between particular types of insecure attachment and aggressive behaviour. Because attachment is one of the most prevalent special needs issues faced by adoptive families, these findings may be a useful piece of the puzzle for those parenting an adopted child with conduct disorder.

Dr. Marlene Moretti is a consultant to the Response Program, which runs out of the Maples in Burnaby. A Registered Psychologist and Associate Professor in Psychology at Simon Fraser University, Dr. Moretti has co-authored several papers on Maples programs and the treatment of conduct disorder from an attachment-based perspective. She kindly agreed to share her insight on these issues first hand, and to elaborate on specific implications for adoptive parents.

What is Conduct Disorder?

DR. MORETTI: The central aspect of a definition of conduct disorder is a severe pattern of repeated violations of basic rights of others. The child may be physically cruel to people or animals, destructive to property, lies and cheats in an instrumental way (not just to avoid being hurt).... There's skipping school, running away from home, theft, threatening to harm others, shoplifting, B and E's.... Conduct disorder, if it persists into adulthood, is called an antisocial personality disorder. That diagnosis has some similar symptoms, although in adults there's usually considerable involvement with the law.

Multi-Modal Treatments

SNAP: In terms of interventions for these children and their families, you've been referring to multi-modal approaches.

DR. MORETTI: I think what's generally accepted now is that the most effective programs are going to help support the child in their family, and in the various contexts that they have to function in. Social skills training, particularly for the younger child, is going to be helpful. Parent management training, again for the younger child because that's when that's most helpful. Working with the schools to understand the learning style of the child; helping the child engage in community activities.... All of these components are where children have to function and you have to look at providing them with support. Most parents in fact do all the time—in all these different aspects of the child's life. For example, you get them on the baseball team, but these kids are different because they end up needing a lot more help to stay on that baseball team—and sometimes people don't want them.

SNAP: Many of our families have encountered that experience—*where is there left to go if nobody wants your child any more?* But it sounds like a multi-modal approach such as BC's Response Program involves people in all those different areas of the child's life....

DR. MORETTI: The program is based on the view that you need an integrated broad-based approach. You need to do a full, comprehensive front-end assessment of how the child is functioning—in the family, in school, in the community—and then help put together a plan of care that will be fairly flexible so that it responds to the child's needs. But the Response Program is a little bit different than the other multi-modal programs in the sense that it takes attachment as a framework for understanding what interventions might be effective.

The Attachment Connection

SNAP: Attachment is certainly a core issue for many adoptive families. Can you explain further how attachment comes into play with conduct disorder?

DR. MORETTI: One simple way of understanding attachment is that basically, all individuals construct a representation—a view of themselves—in the world and their social relationships. And so they come to view themselves in a particular way, and to view others as likely to interact with them in particular ways. A healthy child in a healthy environment comes to view themselves as having positive features, and others as being generally pretty competent in meeting their needs and as fairly responsive to them.

So when they are in need, they feel they can approach others and people will be fairly effective in helping them. For children who haven't had these experiences, their view represents what their experiences have been, which may be that others have not been reliable or that others are perhaps going to abandon them when they're distressed—and these are not conscious kinds of ideas, just an understanding of the world that we all have.

The conduct disordered child will often engage their caregivers by acting in ways that their caregivers cannot avoid responding to. They may appear coercive, and they can be quite aggressive—and a lot of times when a kid's being aggressive, it feels like you're being pushed away. If your child tells you they don't love you, or they hit you, or they run away from you—it doesn't tend to engage people in positive ways. But often the aggressive behaviour is actually a strategy to get others to connect with them—this is the way the child has learned to get a reluctant caregiver to respond. They *have* to respond. Or the child may flip over to being babyish, immature, and very young—"you have to save me" kind of presentation. You might get the same kid doing both of these things—being coercive and babyish—within the same day...for the young child, hitting the parent, pushing and screaming, and then laying down on the ground and crying like a baby. It can be pretty confusing for the caregiver.

Fearful and Preoccupied

What we have found with the children we see—unfortunately, by the time they get to us, they're adolescents—but we found that most predominant styles of attachment are what we call the *fearful style* and the *preoccupied style.*

The fearful child thinks very negatively of themselves and has a very low sense of self-worth. They also view others as very likely to reject them—the sense that others don't like them, just don't care, or that others will harm them. So these children generally avoid others. The preoccupied child is just that, preoccupied—almost desperately seeking others to somehow provide for them. They have the sense that others could provide for them, *could* take care of them, if only they could do what it is their caregivers might want of them. These children can be very clingy and they are very sensitive to rejection.

SNAP: Does each type act out in a different way?

DR. MORETTI: The fearful kids are harder to engage initially. There will be, for instance, more distance and more avoidance. It's harder to cultivate a relationship—they're more likely to complicate the relationship, anticipating that the caregiver is going to check out eventually or hurt them. Trust comes very slowly, if at all.

The preoccupied child is the kind of child who meets their caregiver and bang! *"This is going to be the most wonderful relationship!"* And you're kind of glued together—you probably have the most wonderful honeymoon period, and there's that expectation that you're the most wonderful caregiver who's ever been in their life... And then you're not!

So each type has a different approach to relationships. But ultimately both are similar. In the end, the child feels, in their view, that this person is not really going to be there for them—that they themselves are lacking in some very basic way.

Diagnosis

SNAP: How does one go about getting a diagnosis of conduct disorder? Well-meaning people may be very quick to label without having a real diagnosis— *"Oh, the kid's acting out, s/he must have conduct disorder."*

DR. MORETTI: It's a disorder that requires particular features, and so like all other disorders, there are diagnostic specifications. There's a list of various problem behaviours. You can get children who are diagnosed with conduct disorder for different reasons. The diagnosis simply tells you is that this child, relative to other children, is having very severe behaviour problems. It doesn't tell you anything else about *why* those problems exist.

I really encourage people to go beyond the diagnosis because it alone does not offer a solution to the problem. Look at the behaviour. What is the problem? Why is the child doing this? How long have they been doing this? How many different problem behaviours are there? What different contexts do they occur in? And deal with it that way.

Be Proactive

As parents, I think most of us naturally watch our children to see changes in their behaviour. When we think, something's going wrong—it's not just a bad day or a bad week, it's getting to be a bad month, and this behaviour's just out of control—that's the level that people can sound the alarm on, rather than waiting for a child to be diagnosed.

There are all sorts of things that can be done proactively at that level that are helpful. This can involve providing support for the child and talking about what the problems are, maintaining that relationship, and doing all those things to prevent the relationship from snowballing to a more difficult level—talking to the school, finding out what's going on in the classroom. Is there a problem with the teacher, or with the particular peers in the class? Sometimes it can be a difficult year for the child. Is the child not keeping up with the social skills that are demanded at that level? Is there some support they can get for social skill development? Are there qualified professionals through the schools or elsewhere to help get the child to that next level? If the child has to make that next leap to catch up with their peer group and they're not making it, they're usually really suffering and it takes a real sense of scaffolding them up—and they do get there, but it's important to help them make that jump if it appears that after considerable attempts on their part they are not able to do it on their own.

Go in with Open Eyes

SNAP: What about families whose child comes into the placement already having big problems? Where it's not a matter of catching it early—maybe the problems started in a previous placement. There might be that honeymoon period you talked about where it all looks like it's going to be OK, and then bang, it's over, and suddenly the parents are completely overwhelmed.

DR. MORETTI: I think that probably the most important issue is for adoptive parents to know what they're getting into—to the extent that they can. This is probably the single most frequent recommendation that we make for these children in terms of the caregiving. Because when we see a child who's been through, or burnt through, a number of placements, you're likely to see a child who's extremely demanding, and will continue to be demanding—and it is going to be difficult. So it's coming to accept that is the way it will be, and having realistic expectations for the behaviour of the child.

That in itself just turns down the volume tremendously, in terms of the pressure on the caregiver and the child. If there's the expectation that it's going to be a "happy family thing," the tolerance is going to be pretty low and it's going to have a really big meaning when the child does things that are not consistent to that view. Going into it with open eyes or trying to come to terms with it early on, I think, are really important.

Having clearness and boundaries about what the expectations are, without being punitive, can be really helpful. Try to avoid the power struggle, because many of these children are *not* going to allow a new person to come in and parent them—even though they may give you the impression that this is what they want and need. They're scared that's it's not necessarily a very safe thing for them to allow.

You have to work with where the child is developmentally, and with what they will permit psychologically. Often, for example, it'll be working with the child in negotiation skills, rather than assuming a power position with the child—talking about different action plans, how could this be a positive thing or maybe a not so positive thing for the child to do, laying out options within a structure as you might do for a younger child...when things do happen, as much as possible, trying not to react in the moment and providing ways for people to calm down and debrief afterwards, empathizing with them... The central motivation for the caregiver is being concerned and caring for the welfare of the child rather than rules and solid obedience.

Being A Safe Place

And there's going to be children—such as some of the ones we see—that *cannot* become a part of a big, happy family. But you can be a safe place for them. That may be as much as you can achieve with that child, but it's very, very important for them. It may feel like you're really failing at everything else, because these kids take off and might not be coming home for days and you're concerned about their safety and all of that—but there's nothing short of locking the child up that's going to keep them at home.

Redefine Achievements

SNAP: For a lot of our families, it's been about realigning their expectations about what a family is, what parenting is.... The children's behaviour is often beyond the realm of what they expected or have previously experienced.

DR. MORETTI: It's something where parents really need a lot of support. It's helpful to ask yourself, what would you expect for a child who hasn't had these experiences or expectations in terms of their development? Maybe we need to reconsider what we consider to be achievements. If the child comes back after running away, maybe this can be viewed as a positive step. The caregiver may feel that they're being used, but another way of looking at it is, the child feels safe enough to come back. It doesn't mean that people don't have to have limits and shouldn't be clear about what they can live with. Not at all. But it's just another way of doing it—really trying to avoid getting in this role of being the disciplinarian.

SNAP: That often compounds the problem for children with conduct disorder, doesn't it?

DR. MORETTI: Clarity, structure and clear consequences are helpful—it's really the affect, I think, that these children object to. What's so damaging is that these children often misunderstand what a parent would naturally do as a disciplinary act to a child. For example, for a child where there's a fairly secure attachment, there's more of an ability for that child to understand discipline as something that's in their best interests. But for children who are not securely attached, an act like that may be attributed as being a real act of rejection and abandonment. So you're always having to reframe and explain.

Therapeutic Parenting

SNAP: Do you have any further suggestions for parents who want to address the underlying attachment issue? You touched on a lot of things in terms of parenting— are there other treatments or interventions that parents could consider?

DR. MORETTI: Basically, a lot of the intervention with the parents themselves is their relationship with that child. Attachment isn't something that is born in a permanent form and is completely unchanging—it's a process. It sets a way of seeing things, and then new experiences are gradually integrated. I think the more traumatic the experiences have been in the past, the more difficult it is to integrate different experiences. But if the parents understand that it can be a therapeutic experience—that talking through their relationship with their child and giving that child an opportunity to have a different relationship with an adult is itself a very powerful intervention.

What the research shows with other interventions is that the basic ones— social skills training and parent management—are much more effective for the younger child than they are for the adolescent. If it's a parent who's adopted a young child, by that I mean pre-eight or nine years old, these things can be very helpful. When you get to the older children who've had a longer history of difficult experiences, interventions like social skills training are less effective.

Therapy for Grief and Loss

SNAP: What about grief and loss issues? Would those come into the attachment model as well?

DR. MORETTI: Absolutely. There is a role for family work and individual work with children, in terms of children who have been traumatized, abused, and have had significant losses. For the younger child, play therapy is often useful, and for the older children—who are often emotionally immature in many ways—semi-play therapy, expression-based therapy like art therapy or drama therapy, and these types of things work well. The capacity to benefit from therapy varies from one child to another. But I think you have to hold out the opportunity and see how a child does. Often therapy can be a very important part of things. And sometimes they're not ready and you have to try again at a later time.

SNAP: Is there sometimes the problem of the therapist seeming like yet another authority figure in the eyes of a child with conduct disorder?

DR. MORETTI: The way that I explain therapists to conduct-disordered kids is that it's like finding a pair of shoes that fits. You keep going, you have to try on a lot of pairs, and you have to find the ones that you like and the ones that fit. If you give them choice, and they don't feel as though they've been coerced or tricked, you're going to have much better success. Now that doesn't mean you don't have to give them a lot of support and structure—because left to their own, they won't get there. It's that very fine line—that's the thing when parenting these children, there's not much room to walk in the open spaces!

Prognosis

SNAP: What about prognosis? Some of the literature suggests it's pretty grim, but I've also read that it's more hopeful when early interventions are in place.

DR. MORETTI: It's really mixed. In the literature, a lot of the prognosis is on untreated children. Because there haven't been good systematic evaluations of long-term outcome, it's difficult to know the long-term prognosis. What is generally believed is that early onset, wide-range behaviour problems—when you're seeing early onset behaviour problems across a broad range of contexts—in the home, at school, and with peers—these children are pretty high risk. What this should tell us is that these children really need help early on. That's obviously going to affect the prognosis.

The later, adolescent onset conduct disorder has a better prognosis. About fifty percent of youth with conduct disorder make it out of it. But of all the disorders, the stability of this disorder is quite pronounced. It means you need to do something about it, because if you let it go, children don't grow out of it—that's what people should understand. Don't let it go!

Healthy Adolescent Rebellion

SNAP: I think there's that image we have of wild adolescence, and sometimes we use that to explain the behaviour away...

DR. MORETTI: That's true. In adolescence, typically at about age fifteen, you're going to see children who will go through a lot of pushing and questioning about their parents' values, and opposing their parents. It peaks at age fifteen, and then by about seventeen or eighteen, young people actually come back to the values of their parents. Not completely, of course, but closer in line. That's a normative process and shouldn't be confused with the makings of a conduct disorder. This phase of adolescence does not necessarily involve engagement in aggressive or delinquent behaviour, but it may involve experimenting with different peer groups, values and behaviours. You don't want to overreact. In fact, you want to support your child in exploring their autonomy in all of this. I think what's happening cognitively to children at that age is they are coming into the ability to contrast their position with their parents' position and their peers' position, and there's a lot of diversity there—they are commonly not able at that point to actually integrate it all. And you've got to help them with that. But this is not conduct disorder.

Also, adolescent substance exploration—exploration being some amount of drinking, maybe some amount of drug use, a minimal amount and certainly not doing it on their own, but usually with the peer group—is a normative process. And it's not necessarily something that parents want to condone, but they shouldn't be trotting their child off to a psychiatrist because there is a little bit of this.

SNAP: But parents do get concerned.

DR. MORETTI: Yes. It's really hard to know what's going on. And parents do use their own experiences of what they were like when they were adolescents. Sometimes that for them is what is acceptable. And sometimes they want to make sure that doesn't happen to their child under any circumstances and they overreact the other way!

Actually, attachment helps to understand that process as well—the transgenerational process. Often experiences that an individual has had with their own parents come to be significant in their relationship with their child. What seems to be the case is that parents who have an awareness of that—who can reflect on the experiences of their childhood and have worked some of that through—have a better chance of not repeating that with their own children.

Adoption and Kinship Ties

Another significant question is how you manage this child in their relationship with their biological parents, from an attachment perspective. Often, when we have parents with adopted children come to the program, it's a real significant issue—for foster parents too. Often, parents will describe that contact with the biological parents as very distressing for the child. And the information they have is there to protect the child—particularly if there's been a history of neglect or abuse.

But often the relationship with the parents continues on anyway for the child, regardless of whether the parent is physically present in their life or not. That relationship is there, and the child does go through dealing with it. Sometimes when they don't have contact with the parent—and even when they do—they create a very idealized image of their biological parent. They may be trying desperately to hold on to this view that somehow this parent *could* care for them—it's just circumstances beyond the parent's control. And sometimes it is, which has resulted in the situation they're in. But this idealization may result in playing the one parent off the other parent.

All I can say is, if you can try to understand, from the child's point of view, what they're trying to integrate in their mind and the difficulties this might entail, it is usually better. Idealization is often an attempt on the child's part to hold on to an image that they desperately need to support their self-esteem. It is important to try to support the child in dealing with this as they come to terms with the situation—that it's neither good nor bad, but this is just the way this is. Preventing a child from interacting with and exploring their fantasies about their parents can often promote even greater idealization and this will create difficulties for the child and all caregivers who are involved.

SNAP: Under B.C.'s new adoption act, more openness is encouraged, because studies have shown that more openness is a positive thing for the child and other members of the adoption circle. Nevertheless, a lot of adoptive parents have an initial, protective reaction. And at times openness can be distressing for the adoptive parent, particularly if their child has special needs.

DR. MORETTI: Or if the biological parent has contact and is not terribly consistent on following through on agreements that they've made. It's difficult for adoptive parents, particularly if they feel that somehow their relationship with the child is at risk.

It takes really special people to be able to go through that and hang tough with these kids, but even the difficult times—and maybe particularly the difficult times—can be very significant in bringing children and parents closer together.

The Clinical Psychology Centre at Simon Fraser University is a training centre for graduate students who are completing M.A. and Ph.D. degress in Clinical Psychology. A limited number of referrals are accepted from the community for adult and child, individual, group, couple and family therapy. Play therapy is also offered. The service is not appropriate for crisis or acute needs intervention. Further information is available by contacting (604) 291-4720.

This article originally appeared in the SNAP newsletter, Vol. 14 #1, spring 1998. © 1998 Society of Special Needs Adoptive Parents

abuse
& neglect

I DON'T THINK MANY PEOPLE
REALIZE HOW 'DAMAGED' A
CHILD FREED FOR ADOPTION
MAY BE, PARTICULARLY IF
THEY'VE BEEN ABUSED OR
NEGLECTED.
    – Adopted person &
    social worker

The Realities of Adopting an Older Child:

What You Should Know About Older Children & Abuse

by Joan McNamara

When I was growing up, children worried about monsters under the bed and things that went bump in the dark. Today, children ask their parents about other kinds of monsters: drugs, AIDS, nuclear war, and sexual abuse. Are these things merely a new set of "bogie men" to scare children and worry parents, or do they really have the potential to touch our lives in personal ways?

One of these scary things is sexual abuse, and it does touch the lives of children and families in personal and tragic ways. It has been estimated that one out of every four girls and one out of every five boys will experience some form of sexual abuse before age 18. That figure does not include statistics for date rape.

The Statistics About Older Children

For adoptive families the statistics are more worrisome. It has been estimated that more than 75 percent of children moving from foster care to adoption have experienced sexual abuse. This is a phenomena that is not limited to the United States and Canada, but unfortunately extends to children from other countries adopted by North American families as well.

It also is important to be aware that some situations and characteristics make children more vulnerable to abuse, even after they move into safe, loving adoptive homes. Some of these factors are related to the child's experience before adoption or to characteristics that cause the child to be perceived as more vulnerable.

Unfortunately, the reality of sexual abuse as a potential threat to our child's physical and emotional safety is not an invention of pessimistic adoption workers or paranoid parent activists. But there are things we can do as parents to protect children, to reduce the possibilities of harm, to encourage self-esteem, safety skills, and a sense of competence to help children heal from trauma and break the cycles of abuse.

Parenting Older Children

As parents, the first thing we can do to help our children is become informed. We need to know what sexual abuse is, what makes children more likely to be abused and to experience trauma, and what helps children in the healing process. In addition, we need to look within ourselves to our own feelings about sexuality and abuse and to our own experiences. It is harder to reach out to children and help them with pain if we are unwilling to ask for help for ourselves when we need it.

Child sexual abuse is not just the violence of rape. It can involve any interaction, even without direct contact, where a child is being used for the sexual stimulation of another person or exposed to sexuality before the child is developmentally ready. This inappropriate interaction between a child and another person in a power position does not have to be between the child and an adult, it could be with another child. It does not have to involve a male or someone of the opposite sex; it does not have to be someone bigger or stronger or older than the child. The person, child or adult, male or female, in the power position could be someone intellectually or emotionally dominant instead of (or in addition to being) physically dominant.

A child who is allowed to witness sexual intercourse or explicit pornography has experienced one form of sexual abuse. So have children who have been told that they are no good and untrustworthy because they are male and all men are undependable and abusive. A girl who learns that she has little value except as a sexual object for others develops negative self-esteem and a skewed sense of sexuality and sexual roles.

All of these children can grow up feeling hopeless and helpless about what they have experienced and what life holds for them in the future. They can develop identities as victims, powerless to make changes, instead of as survivors, people who have hope for themselves and others.

Parents can encourage survivor traits for their children, especially through opportunities to build three key skills: the ability to form genuine reciprocal relationships, the ability to empathize with another and express it altruistically, and a sense of hope and optimism. Children who have had poor or broken attachments find it more difficult to understand and develop these three skills.

Bonding with an Older Child

Adoption theories have emphasized attachment and bonding as a way for adoptions to succeed. But traumatized children must first build or rebuild some of the foundations that make these possible, especially a sense of trust. Attachment is not the method but the end goal for many adopted children. In the adoptive family this starts with the basics first: physical needs for survival met dependably, such as regular meals, a warm house; safety needs reinforced, such as protection from harm, security of the same rules and routines, and consistency of caretakers.

Most children have these two basic needs met in infancy and thus learn to trust and hope. Traumatized children may have had these building blocks of emotional development shattered if these were even in place to begin with. Some children moving into adoptive families may have such difficulty with making genuine relationships because trauma, broken or missing attachments, or poor parenting have not given them these building blocks that they are said to have an attachment disorder. These children may be reluctant to trust or hope. They may have problems re-establishing attachments, or they may be so unable to do this that only intensive therapeutic work holds any promise of developing these abilities.

It is only after children have made some gains toward establishing firm foundations in the basics that they can trust enough to reach out. This is where belonging starts and love may be able to take root.

Effects of Childhood Trauma

Childhood trauma such as sexual abuse can damage, delay, or prevent these foundations from becoming stable. The harm that is done to children who experience sexual abuse is not just physical, but the harm occurs by introducing confusing issues to children before they are ready for them. Sexual abuse most often damages children's sense of trust in themselves and in the world; it leaves them with a skewed sense of sexuality, their own and in general. Sexually abused children often have difficulty with personal boundaries because they have been taught by the invasive experience of abuse that their own boundaries are not respected.

Something very personal, central to their sense of identity, individuation, and developing sexuality has been violated. This can affect the way children perceive intimacy (how much they allow people to be close) and control (how much they trust others to help). Some children have difficulty understanding and respecting other people's boundaries and respecting and protecting their own because of these issues.

One Child's Experience

Joshie was a 6-year-old boy whose trouble with boundaries made it difficult for his classmates and kindergarten teacher. Joshie would take things from other children's desks and sit so close to others that they felt their space invaded. He would touch his teacher constantly, sometimes on the breasts.

These boundary issues also made life complicated for Joshie himself. Joshie expected that others would take his things too. He let another child in the class wear his new coat home. And he allowed a bigger boy at recess to pull down his pants. In his classroom playhouse Joshie asked a girl to touch his penis and anus and tried to force her to allow him to touch her inside her underwear.

Joshie didn't have a sense of where his body finished and someone else's territory or personal space began. He felt that others would probably hurt him, and he felt he couldn't defend himself well since he was supposed to be hurt. Joshie learned these lessons, and lost his sense of self, through the experience of being sexually abused at age 3. The abuse taught Joshie that he didn't have the right to his own personal boundaries, external and internal. His right to set and keep the boundaries that determine the amount of sharing and closeness in relationships was damaged, on physical, sexual, emotional, and even spiritual levels. Joshie didn't have much of the sense of hope and awe about the universe and his place in it that is part of the spiritual development of young children.

Living Together

There are no crystal balls or magic formulas to use to help children and families heal and grow together. Each child's experiences, responses, and potentials combined with a particular family's unique gifts and skills make a complex and highly individual design of possibilities. We do know, however, that these challenges involve hard work over time, best accomplished with support for child, parent, and family. Like the art of creating a tapestry, the tangles and knots are sometimes most obvious as we work. Often it is only much later that we can see the beauty of the pattern we have touched, with all its dark and bright.

Warning Signs

Parents want to know how to tell if their child has been traumatized. Adults often can't tell for sure, especially if a child cannot or will not share about these experiences.

Many of the symptoms that traumatized children may display are not obvious. Some are similar to those that indicate other types of childhood upset, for example, bedwetting or nightmares. No one symptom or behavior is an absolute signal of trauma, past or present. The more symptoms, however, especially those related to sexuality, the more likely the child has experienced sexual abuse. The greater the number of symptoms and the more intense and lasting their display, the deeper the impact of his trauma is likely to be for a child. These are merely some of the indicator of problems.

Some common symptoms of childhood trauma:
- High levels of anxiety; low frustration tolerance.

- Difficulty with concentration; spacing out or daydreams.
- Victim stance: helpless, hopeless, limited sense of responsibility or control.
- Flashbacks, intrusive memories, fantasies relating to abuse, violence, or sex.
- Phobic behavior.
- Difficulty with cause and effect, decision-making, and learning from consequences.
- Self-destructive, accident prone, helpless behavior.
- Oppositional, disobedient behavior, difficulty with authority.
- Passive, overly compliant, or babyish behavior.
- Consistent lying; stealing.
- Firesetting; cruelty to animals.
- Compulsive behaviors: eating disorders, drugs, repetitive ritual, nail biting, etc.

Some common child sexual abuse symptoms:
- Bedwetting; daytime wetting.
- Soiling; intestinal problems.
- Detachment from body sensations and feelings.
- Frequent urinary, genital, or anal infections or itching.
- Somatic or stress-related problems.
- Vomiting or gagging without organic causes.
- Overeating, gorging; difficulty eating or swallowing.
- Seductive, provocative, or overtly sexual behavior.
- Firesetting, cruelty to animals.
- Poor hygiene; dressing in layers; compulsive behaviors.
- Inordinate fear of adults, male and/or female.
- Sexual themes in conversation or play.
- Boundary problems; self-destructive or aggressive.
- Sexual behavior in response to stress; frequent masturbation.
- Sexual knowledge/behavior beyond age or developmental level.

This article originally appeared in *OURS* magazine, March/April 1993, pp. 24-26. It is reprinted here with permission of the author.

When Your Child Has Been Abused:

These Parenting Pointers Can
Help Your Family Deal with Pain

by Joan McNamara

Children who have been abused and neglected usually have a lot of anxiety and confused or negative emotions. Abused children usually have not learned effective and acceptable ways of dealing with their difficult emotions. Instead, they may have a repertoire of defenses that may have been important survival skills before but are out of place or unacceptable now in their families.

Your Home

Your home may be the first place your child feels safe enough to risk talking about feelings and events. You can encourage feelings of safety by the way you respond to your child. You may be able to help your child feel safe and secure with you, your family, and also with him or herself in a number of ways:

1. Express acceptance of what your child tells you. Even if you are not sure the facts are accurate or you disagree, what your child tells you is the reality for your child. To tell your daughter who is already feeling vulnerable that she shouldn't feel that way or that an event took place in April, not June, is to tell her that she is wrong.

2. Put aside your feelings. Sexuality and sexual abuse are difficult issues for everyone. You may feel uncomfortable, embarrassed, shocked, unsure, disgusted, angry, or scared. All are legitimate feelings, but we must put our own needs aside temporarily so we can sensitively help children deal with theirs. Fear of adult reactions is one of the major reasons children don't break the secrecy surrounding sexual abuse.

3. Give children permission to have feelings. Model appropriate verbal and nonverbal ways to express feelings in your family, and specifically teach children what these are. Teach children that feelings are okay, even giant, scary ones, but there are ways of expressing these that can help you, not hurt you. Teach your child what the consequences are for behaviors.

4. Allow children to take control in safe, appropriate ways that reinforce success and positive self-esteem, such as making decisions appropriate to their developmental, emotional level (which can be different from their chronological age). Ask your child to tell you when and how much body contact such as hugs

or lap sitting he or she would like. At the same time, provide a dependable and reliable structure that includes clearly defined tasks and schedules.

5. Help your child feel he or she is not alone. Sadly, a lot of children get hurt in the same way your child did. Being with a group of children who have been abused is a good way to begin healing, not only because it's an effective therapeutic approach but also because a child can begin to feel less isolated and alienated.

6. Tell your child you feel sad that he or she was hurt but glad you can both talk about it. Tell your child that your love will not change even if terrible, yucky things happen to him or her.

Dealing with Difficult Behaviors

Children who have been abused respond in various ways, but some behaviors are more difficult to deal with than others. Children may tell you about the abuse in public such as at the supermarket. Will you be embarrassed, shocked, flustered, or angry? Children may feel safer divulging information in public where you are less likely to make a scene or in some way hurt them.

If this happens, tell your child that you want to talk, but not now. Express this in a way that reassures your child you are not running away from the issue. Most parents have had the experience of children bringing up sensitive issues with them as the children are about to leave for the school bus or while the parents have both hands on the steering wheel of their car and their eyes on the road.

Children who have been sexually abused may act out in sexual ways. They may be repeating what they have been taught by the abuser. They may have been "eroticized" by premature exposure to sexuality.

When well-meaning adults talk to children about "bad touch" and "bad people" and how it must have been a terrible experience, these adult words and assumptions may have a disconcerting effect on children for whom some parts of the abuse served as survival or pleasure functions. As difficult as it is to understand or accept, parts of the sexual abuse experience may have had positive rewards for the child, even though other parts were quite frightening or painful. The abuse gave the child attention with promises of being made "special." In the logic of the child, if adults label the experience as "bad" but the child felt good about some of it, doesn't that mean that the child is bad too?

Children need to know they can have more than one emotion and that our bodies are made to respond in certain ways, whether or not we want them to. Children need to know that things that are not appropriate or hurt can look or feel good at the same time, and that grownups make mistakes. Explain how it's sad that the people they counted on to take care of them didn't do a good job; but then explain it's possible to love someone still, even after they do hurtful things, even if you are angry or hate them at the same time.

Children who masturbate excessively or in public places will need to be given guidelines about what is acceptable behavior and where and when to do it. Children need to be told that wanting to touch yourself is a natural feeling, but that there are social and family rules about this behavior.

For other children, touching themselves may bring reminders of the abuse. Parents and therapists can work with children to explain that this can happen when children are introduced to stages and behaviors in sexuality before they are developmentally ready and help children work through these feelings and behaviors to regain a positive sense of control and self-esteem. Some techniques that are used with children are allowing children to vent their anger and fear about the abuse in safe and appropriate ways; finding acceptable ways for children to gain a sense of appropriate power and control; developing alternative patterns to deal with stress; and creating new images and scripts for children to practice when dealing with sexual, angry, sad, and scared feelings.

Some children try to regain a sense of control or power that was taken from them by abuse by trying to control others. Sexual abuse of children by children, like rape, is less about sexual pleasure and more about power and rage. It can become a compulsive behavior to deal with low self-esteem, extreme pain, and the need to control. Children who develop a victim stance of chronic helplessness and hopelessness may move into victimizing behaviors more easily if they have poor impulse control, limited conscience, and few coping mechanisms to deal with frustration and pain. Children with attachment problems, who have not had many opportunities to develop a functioning conscience yet can have strong feelings of rage, may be a higher risk for sexually abusive behavior.

Children who abuse other children or pets need immediate and on-going help with the family and therapeutic interventions in order to break out of these destructive patterns. The traditional form of individual, confidential therapy may be the least helpful for both traumatized children moving into adoptive families and for children who sexually perpetrate. Family work and group work can be much more helpful, particularly in dealing with the secrecy issues that sexual abuse often brings. Sexual abuse and the residue of sexual abuse, such as abusive behaviors by the victims, thrive on secrecy. Open communication can be a part of the work that begins to break these patterns.

Confusing Feelings
Children who experience sexual abuse at a very young age, or children who have blanked out their conscious memories of the abuse, may not have any visual cues

or symbols to relate to their confusing feelings. In a manner of speaking, they have no framework in which to fit their feelings and figure them out. This can make the work of healing very difficult.

Sharing that these are normal feelings for kids who have been abused, since being abused can leave a child with lots of strong and confusing feelings, can help children feel that they are not crazy. Talking in very general terms of what might have happened to cause these feelings, based on what other kids have talked about, can give them a beginning for understanding and healing.

Children who have experienced abuse usually have difficulty trusting new people. They have difficulty sharing intimate feelings. They may not know where their feelings have come from, and they may not remember the event. This complicates things, especially when the feelings involved with sexual abuse are confusing enough to deal with. Children may feel shame. They may be angry, even filled with rage, although they may suppress it. They may be afraid, especially if the abuser threatened them in some way.

Children need to know that their bodies were meant to respond to touch, even if they don't want them to. It's normal for some parts of sexual abuse to feel pleasurable or confusing. That sometimes happens, but children are not ready yet for all kinds of touch, especially grown-up touching.

Many children, even if the facts are public, do not want to talk about their experiences of sexual abuse. They may deny or minimize the facts and feelings about their own abuse, or they may even retract previous statements they have made. Even though this can slow the work of healing, it is a natural reaction to pain.

Some children are afraid to talk because they still fear that the abuser has some power over them. They fear people will reject them. Sexually abused children may think they are disgusting and that they are bad.

Taking on the blame is a common reaction children can have to negative experiences because in many ways it both validates the bad feelings they are left with and gives back a sense of control. For some children, repeating abusive situations, either acting as a victim or as a victimizer, is one way they attempt to regain a sense of control and reinforcement that they are bad.

Helping your Child

You can help your child in a number of ways. You can define acceptable behaviors, model these and talk about them directly, and set specific limits. For example, say that in your house, dads don't hurt children or touch their private parts, and no one else is allowed to either; in this family children aren't allowed to hit or to take things that belong to others.

Then talk about what is allowed and encourage these behaviors often. For example, children and parents share "okay" touching such as hugs, lap-sitting, and backrubs. Clearly explain how these behaviors are positive and help people feel good and grow healthy. Sexually abused children may misinterpret these behaviors or discount them since they may have had few experiences of positive physical touch.

In addition to setting limits, you can encourage children to do what's right. These verbal messages can encourage-positive behaviors and self-esteem in children:

- Because people didn't always take care of you, you didn't get to learn about appropriate touch and how to share feelings the right way. We'll help you with that.
- In this family, children don't share grown-up touching; instead these other types of touching are the kind that help children share and grow.
- That kind of touching is okay for children; it makes them feel good inside.
- You are doing a good job learning about touching, even if you don't always get it right.
- You can make mistakes, and I will keep on loving you.
- That was a great hug. It makes me feel good, and I can carry that feeling around inside me for the rest of the morning. Thank you.
- Which kind of attention do you need right now? How can you get it in good ways?
- I care about you so I won't let you hurt yourself or others. You are not ready yet for this situation, but you will be eventually since you are working on these issues.
- You are a smart person, and you will be able to learn about how to handle feelings and behaviors. We'll help you until you are ready, and even after that we'll be there if you need help again.
- Lots of children who have been hurt remember their abuse or have thoughts and feelings about sex when they get close to people. Some of it may feel scary, some of it may feel exciting. If this happens for you we can talk about it and help you figure out ways to deal with it.
- Sometimes children who have been abused get confused between good touch and sexual touch. We don't give children sexual or inappropriate touch, but sometimes it may feel like that to you. If that happens, that's normal. Let us know, so we can help you figure it out and work with the feelings.
- I'm glad you are my child. I like sharing good touch, and I like helping you learn about sharing good loving. I don't always like your mistakes, but I enjoy seeing you learn from them. I like watching you grow.

Yes, parenting a child who has been abused can be difficult. But by providing a structured home environment with open communication that encourages your child to feel safe, you begin the journey of healing.

This article originally appeard in *OURS* magazine, July/August 1993, pp.22-24. It is reprinted here with permission of the author.

Parents Ask About Sexual Abuse & Sexuality of Young People with Disabilities
by Jane Holland & Karen Van Rheenen

In order to help protect their children from sexual abuse, parents of children with disabilities ask a number of questions:

What is sexual abuse?
Sexual abuse is any sexual exploitation of a person, whether consensual or not. It includes touching of a sexual nature and sexual intercourse. It may include any behaviour of a sexual nature toward a child or adolescent.

How common is sexual abuse?
An estimated one in four girls and one in ten boys will experience some form of sexual abuse before the age of 18. Studies indicate that between 39% and 68% of girls and between 16% and 30% of boys with intellectual impairments will be sexually abused before the age of 18.

What makes young people with disabilities more vulnerable to sexual abuse?
- Not knowing enough to recognize or report abuse;
- Being taught to be passive and to obey all adults without question;
- Never getting a chance to learn to make decisions that boost self-confidence;
- Not having friends -- lonely young people may do anything just to receive some attention and affection.

What are the signs of sexual abuse?
Many young people with disabilities cannot tell us that they have been sexually abused. Others are too afraid to speak out. Some do not realize that they have a right to refuse such abuse.

The only certain signs are pregnancy, sexually transmitted diseases, and vaginal or anal tears. However, much abuse does not involve penetration.

Other signs include changes in behaviour, such as sudden fear of men or certain men, a fear of being left alone with certain individuals, nightmares, bed wetting, thumb sucking, clinging to a parent, precocious sexual behaviour and sexual knowledge.

Is teaching about sexuality really that important for young people with disabilities?

Children with disabilities, like all children, will need to learn to care for and understand their bodies. They will go through biological changes during puberty that may be frightening if they don't understand what is happening. They will be faced with social and sexual decisions and need to be prepared to handle them responsibly and protect themselves.

What should I do to overcome feelings of sadness or fear when I think about sexuality issues related to my child with a disability?

Finding other parents with children with disabilities, good friends with an empathic ear, or a supportive counsellor may help you to better understand and cope with these feelings. Getting the support you need will also help to ensure that your feelings do not impact negatively on your relationship with your child.

How do I start sex education with my child?

Get comfortable by clarifying your own attitudes about sexuality and the information and moral code you wish to teach. Your goal should be to impart a positive, healthy, enriching attitude about the body and sexuality.

Don't wait until your child starts to ask questions; some children never ask. It is helpful to start young -- by labelling body parts, for example. As issues become more complex, focus on functional, usable information rather than technical information about sexuality. Prioritize topics based on the most pressing needs; this will vary according to children's ages and life experiences.

Find books with clear, simple illustrations to explain anatomy. Teach the rules of appropriate touch and social sexual behaviour by example and instruction. Ensure that other people in the child's support network abide by these rules. Encourage questions and discussion, and answer honestly.

How important is social skills training in protecting young people with disabilities from sexual abuse?

Research indicates that a lack of social skills training places young persons with disabilities at greater risk of abuse. The following social skills training is suggested:

- Give children a chance to be with other children.
- Coach them in skills such as how to say hello, who can give them a hug, who they can shake hands with, what to say, differences between public and private, and assertiveness.
- Teach skills step-by-step by deciding what behaviour you want to teach, demonstrating the behaviour, practising the behaviour in private, giving feedback to your child, rewarding good behaviour, and substituting appropriate for inappropriate behaviour.
- Teach them how to make decisions by discussing ways to solve a problem, picking the best solution, demonstrating what to do, having the child practise in a safe environment, and giving feedback.

This article was originally distributed by the Sexual Health Resource Network, McCreary Centre, Sunny Hill Health Centre for Children, and appeared in the SNAP newsletter, Vol. 11 #3, fall 1995. It is reprinted here with permission of the Family Support Institute.

Indicators of Sexual Abuse

Indicators of sexual abuse are not different for children and youth with disabilities. However, sometimes indicators may be mistakenly attributed to manifestations of a young person's disability rather than alerting caregivers to the possibility that sexual abuse is occurring. While many indicators, particularly those of a behavioural nature, may be signs of other problems in a young person's life, a series or cluster of indicators observed over a period of time is cause for concern regarding abuse.

Alice Richard, Coordinator of the Special Needs Program at the Victoria Child Sexual Abuse Society, has developed two lists of particular relevance to young people with disabilities: one for individuals with moderate to severe communication difficulties, and another for individuals with more functional physical and verbal abilities. She notes that:

Individuals with disabilities may exhibit a number of behaviours that can be associated with sexual abuse. How these behaviours manifest themselves will depend largely on the extent of developmental delay and/or the degree of impairment. Persons who are non-verbal generally exhibit more of the physical and behavioural indicators of sexual abuse. If the individual is a survivor of sexual abuse their level of trauma and the indicators will most likely reflect the age or developmental stage they were in when the abuse occurred.

The following indicators will be most likely exhibited by:

Individuals with Moderate to Severe Communication Difficulties
- unusual or extreme fears of certain places in their home or towards certain caregivers with whom they were previously at ease (i.e, phobic or avoidant responses)
- feces smearing
- frequent angry outbursts - e.g., biting or destructive acts
- regressive behaviours
- venereal disease or frequent urinary tract infections
- vaginal or anal trauma
- frantic behaviour during bathing or changing clothes
- noticeable changes in behaviour such as suddenly avoiding a certain person, place or room, and/or obvious discomfort with physical contact
- self-abusive behaviours
- sleep and eating disturbances
- depression
- excessive masturbation (occurring with noticeable frequency) or other types of inappropriate sexual behaviour
- dramatic mood swings
- uncharacteristic outbursts of anger or hostility.

In addition to the above, the following indicators may be exhibited by:

Individuals with More Functional Physical and Verbal Abilities
- comments or drawings which make sense only in a sexual context or which contain sexualized themes
- attempts at sexual behaviour with others, particularly those in less powerful positions
- sexually abusive behaviour toward others
- verbal and/or physical aggression toward others
- isolation from peers - withdrawing from and/or avoiding contact with people with whom they had previous sought contact
- running away - not wanting to return home
- emotional dependency - more than previously demonstrated
- sexual experimentation with age inappropriate partners
- an alarming inability to distinguish between reality and fantasy
- somatic complaints
- performance deterioration
- expressions of guilt or shame
- accident proneness

- an expressed inability to trust others
- an inability to differentiate between platonic male-female relationships and those of a sexual nature
- a disregard or inability to keep oneself "safe" (i.e., frequently puts self in potentially abusive situations)

This article originally appeared in the SNAP newsletter, Vol. 11 #3, fall 1995. © 1995 Society of Special Needs Adoptive Parents

Talking About Sex with Children with Special Needs

by Susan MacRae

Sex. Can anyone talk of a more powerful word in the English language? Sex sells: it sells toothpaste, movies, Cadillacs, beer, Virginia Slims, paperbacks, blue jeans, chewing gum, cologne, T-shirts, fitness clubs, airline tickets—even fast food! ('Increase your cup size' reads an ad for French fries on the side of a bus). Yet, with all the proliferation of sexual images used in the media, how many of us truly understand and know all the scientific and mechanical facts of our bodies? How many of us heard the words *labia, clitoris, scrotum,* and *prostate* explained to us by our parents, teachers, doctors or nurses in our communities when growing up? Or what about the subjects nobody talked about: masturbation, paedophilia, sexually transmitted disease, homosexuality, celibacy or even menopause. And can you imagine how your life might have been (or be?) different if those subjects had been explained more fully to you, with honesty and maturity? Now, imagine yourself trying to sort through all the conflicting messages or lack of information about sex when you have all the urges of a twenty-one year-old body, but the mental capacity of a six year-old!

Like all living creatures on the planet, human bodies follow their own cycles. We are born, and we live, work and love in our communities as we mature and then die. In this age of the HIV/AIDS pandemic, Hepatitis C, as well as breast and testicular cancers, knowledge about our sexual health ensures our bodies' survival. Meg Hickling, in her book *Speaking of Sex: Are You Ready to Answer the Questions Your Kids Will Ask?* tells us that in order to ensure our bodies' survival, we must learn to talk about sex with our children openly, with the correct scientific terminology, from an early age so that we can become sexually mature and loving adults.

Meg Hickling, a registered nurse, has been a sexual health educator in BC for over twenty years. *Speaking of Sex* is a compilation of stories, anecdotes and questions about sex she has encountered in her workshops with children, parents and professionals, including clergy, social workers, lawyers and pharmacists. The book serves as a highly readable handbook on when and how to talk to your kids about sex. It includes a section on the "Basics", as well as sections on each phase of a child's development: preschoolers, primaries, intermediates, adolescents, and adults. Hickling gives straight answers to all the questions a child might ask, ranging from what happens in the doctors' office, to sexually transmitted diseases, to the pregnant teen. She includes a section entitled 'Celebrating Diversity' at the end of her book, so that 'sexuality should be celebrated, that there is a beauty and elegance to it all, that there are rights, responsibilities and choices, and that we are not simply biological creatures, at the mercy of hormonal urges.'

What Your Child Needs to Know (and Why)
For parents of special needs adoptive children, *Speaking of Sex* is a highly valuable resource. In the section 'What a Child Needs to Know', Hickling lists the facts about each stage of development. For example, according to Hickling, a preschool child should know (before attending school):
- the names for genitals: penis, testicles, scrotum, anus, vulva, labia, vagina, clitoris, uterus, ovaries;
- that reproduction happens when a man's sperm joins a woman's ovum by sexual intercourse;
- that the baby grows in the uterus;
- the basics about menses and nocturnal emission as clean and healthy processes; and, not to pick up condoms.

Many parents, upon reading Hicklings' recommendations, will balk at telling their children that much information. "We need to let children be children," they might rationalize, "children must keep their innocence." But, until we learn to teach our children all the facts about our bodies with honesty and maturity, Hickling argues, children will not know their rights and boundaries about their bodies, and hence, fall prey to sexual abuse. Sexual abusers readily admit that they choose their victims according to the communication level which that child might have with the parents in the home. If the abuser thinks that there is a possibility that the child might tell their parents (because the child knows all the words for what is happening to them), then the abuser is less inclined to choose the informed child as a victim. So, in trying to keep their children 'innocent' by withholding information, parents, in effect, may set their children up to lose their innocence much earlier than they would have if the child had been properly informed.

Special Needs

Although all children need to be protected from sexual abuse, whether they are two or twenty, protecting a child with special needs from abuse will be a highly important consideration for adoptive parents because of their child's individual capacities and needs. Even parents who have to provide 24 hour-a-day, 7-day-a-week care will still not always be able to make sure that their child with special needs will always:

(a)   maintain their own privacy and respect others' boundaries;

(b)   be protected from and be aware of sexual abuse; and

(c)   maintain clean sexual health, and use protection should they become sexually active.

According to interviews I conducted with two foster parents, and with Special Education consultant Marie MacRae, the key to educating children with special needs about their sexual health is repetition. A special needs parent who follows Meg Hicklings' guidelines about what a child needs to know and when, will be giving age-appropriate information as special needs children often develop biologically at the same rate as other children. However, whereas the child without special needs might need to be told only once or twice about where babies come from or who it is okay to touch and why, that same information will need to be repeated several times to children with special needs.

Going back to the example in the introduction, we expect a twenty-one year old to have a certain level of maturity and knowledge about their body. But what if that twenty-one year old has the mental capacity of a six year old? How can they be expected to take care of themselves physically, and to understand the consequences and responsibilities of their sexuality without a great deal of repetition? Therefore the parent will have to take a great deal more responsibility for ensuring that their child makes the right choices. A parent can never assume the child with special needs knows more than what they have been told by the parent, because the child will either often forget, or not fully comprehend the information. By repeating information to your child, even a few days or weeks after you have discussed a topic, a parent can ensure open communication about sexuality, as well as double check that their child with special needs will be able to understand the concepts they are learning.

Boundaries

Besides learning about their bodies and sexual health, children with special needs will have to learn very clearly about their boundaries. Many parents adopt children who have an early history of sexual abuse. In the case of sexual abuse and dysfunctional families, physical boundaries between family members have been very blurred. Touch conveys powerful messages about who a child is, and their place in the family. In the case of dysfunctional families, touch has conveyed a powerful negative message to a child's physical, emotional, and spiritual self. Often, by the time a parent adopts a child with special needs who has been sexually abused, the parent will have to go through an entire process of re-learning and changing those powerful messages conveyed about touch to the child.

The Ministry for Children and Families has programs available to parents of special needs children concerning boundary and sexuality issues, including a program called 'Circles'. In the 'Circles' program, kids explore the circles of contacts in their lives: the family circle, the friends/community circle, and the public circle. Colouring exercises and other activities can enhance a child with special needs' understanding of appropriate behaviour within each particular circle. In Kelowna, a program called 'Life Horizons' provides sex education and group exercises for teens with mental challenges. By accessing these programs, a child can begin to know their boundaries. However, as one of the foster parents recommended, a parent should make sure they know who their child talks to about sex, especially in the case of past sexual abuse, as a counsellor must be trained as to how to deal with trauma should a memory arise in the child. As well, in the case of sexually abused children who become intrusive, parents can access a program called 'Pathfinders' through the Ministry to help prevent their child from acting out on others what has been done to them. Again, a parent will need to be pro-active about researching the mental health qualifications of the counsellors, teachers and educators their child comes in contact with.

However, even when a child with special needs grows up in an affectionate household, with lots of hugging and appropriate kissing, a parent can not assume that their child will know that it is not necessarily safe to hug and kiss the teacher or the mailman in the same manner. Children with special needs will often need to be told verbally who it is okay to be affectionate with and why. Touch has its own language, and like speaking, or reading and writing, a child with special needs will need to take more time interpreting both the negatives and positives of the language of touch.

Special needs adoptive parents also need to understand their own as well as their child's boundaries. Whatever their child's functional ability, or past history, an individual's sexual history is private and confidential. Even a parent of a child with special needs will not need to know everything. But they will need to know that their child is safe, protected, and that the child knows their rights when it comes to their own bodies. By being tolerant, informed, and comfortable enough in their own sexuality to talk openly and honestly, as well as being involved in the child's life, a parent can provide the best role model for the future sexual behaviour of all their children, special needs or not.

Self-Esteem and Body Image

Sexual imagery in the media preys upon our self-esteem, and our loveability. The slogan 'increase your cup size' implies that we may not be loveable enough solely because of the size of our sexual organs. Because of an already inherent feeling of alterity or *other*, children with special needs will probably be more affected by the insidious messages about sexuality presented by the media and society. When the need to be loved becomes greater than the need to protect his/herself, then there is cause for alarm, and a potential danger to the child.

Any parent, but most especially special needs parents, need to be vigilant about the messages the child receives about their sexuality and self-esteem. And, because of their child's added vulnerability, they will need to know *who* the people are that the child comes in contact with in their life—a necessity that may last well into adulthood for many of these young people.

Everyone has a need to be loved, comforted and touched. The sexual relationship is one of the chief pleasures of adult life, and one of the greatest opportunities for spiritual growth. A healthy sexuality in *Speaking of Sex* is described as:

- an investment in the partner as an individual, rather than solely as a means of sexual gratification;
- fidelity to promises and agreements;
- mutual interest in types of sexual play'
- non-injury to the partner;
- responsibility for one's actions and for the well-being of the partner. It maintains concern for the significant other, the partner, the family, the society.

By providing good role models as parents and working on our own sexual maturity, and by always keeping communication around sexual issues open and tolerant, we can give children with special needs the opportunity to celebrate a responsible sexuality, and participate in the diversity of life. As Meg Hickling writes: "We must not continue to bring darkness and shame to the world. We must bring light! In fact, we must promote light!"

Meg Hickling's *Speaking of Sex* (Northstone, 1996), and her sequel *More Speaking of Sex* (Northstone, 1999) are available from the SNAP Library.

This article originally appeared in the SNAP newsletter, Vol. 15 #3, fall 1999. © 1999 Society of Special Needs Adoptive Parents

Emotional Abuse:

Giving it a Name, Coping with the Aftermath

by Sara Graefe

Emotional abuse has not been dealt with as consistently or extensively as other forms of abuse in research, literature, and child protection legislation, and pulling together appropriate material is indeed a challenge.

The problem is linked to the elusive nature of emotional abuse. It is far less tangible than either physical or sexual abuse, even though it is often a feature of both. Further, professionals remain stuck in the on-going debate over its definition. Nevertheless, experts in the field agree that emotional abuse is very real, occurring not only in conjunction with other abuse but also on its own. Its impact on children can be devastating. In fact, it is often the aspect of physical and sexual abuse that is the most deeply rooted and hardest to heal. Research has linked psychological maltreatment to problems with attachment, social competence and social adjustment, behaviour, cognitive ability and problem solving, and educational achievement (Hart, Brassard, & Karlson, 1996). The recent implementation of British Columbia's new *Child, Family and Community Services Act* provides a timely opportunity to examine emotional abuse. This groundbreaking new legislation is the first in our province's history that attempts to give emotional abuse a name.

Giving It A Name

Most provinces have now implemented modern legislation which attempts to capture a definition of emotional abuse. The new *CF & CS Act*, which has been in force since January 29, 1996, is B.C.'s first piece of child protection legislation which includes emotional abuse as its own entity. Its inclusion is significant. As Jeremy Berland, who helped draft the legislation, explains, "It was difficult *not* to include it. It's clear that emotional abuse can have a tremendous impact on children. Modern child development theory shows us that belittling children or withholding love, for example, *does* have an effect. Withholding affection goes along with withholding clothing and food, but not always—it's important that it can be recognized in isolation, as well as in conjunction with other types of abuse."

Under the previous Act, criteria under "abuse and neglect" or "deprived through death, absence or disability of parents" could be stretched to include emotional abuse. While this allowed emotional abuse to be considered, the definition was both too broad and too narrow—on one hand, emotionally abused children continued to fall through the cracks, while at the same time, *any* kind of parental behaviour could potentially be labelled as emotionally abusive, without having to be linked to a symptom or sign in the child.

CF&CS Act

The definition in the new Act places an emphasis on the *observable* behaviours in the child that can be *linked* back to the parent's conduct. These behaviours include severe anxiety, severe depression, severe withdrawal, and severe self-destructive or aggressive behaviour. Berland draws special attention to the stipulation *severe*. "It's not a matter of a child just feeling anxious and depressed. A lot of us have felt like that during childhood, and especially adolescence."

The behaviours must be connected to the parents' conduct, to either acts of commission or omission. Emotionally abusive acts of commission include humiliating, scapegoating, denigrating, rejecting, ridiculing, ostracizing and undermining the child's self-esteem through unrealistic expectations. Acts of omission constitute emotional neglect and are characterized by the absence of action, and include parental detachment, emotional indifference, lack of involvement or interest, and affective coldness in relation to the child (Kadushin & Martin, 1988). B.C.'s definition of emotional abuse is in keeping with trends across North America, and follows the suggested American Bar Association Juvenile Justice standard. It is also similar to legislation currently in place in Ontario and Nova Scotia.

In terms of current practice, a child is rarely deemed in need of protection on the basis of emotional abuse alone, as it is usually linked to more tangible types of abuse and neglect which are also outlined in the new Act. Social workers are generally encouraged to rely on these areas first, as expertise in the field of emotional abuse continues to catch up. Further, a finding under the new Act doesn't automatically mean the removal of the child. The Act provides a range of mechanisms which permit the social worker to implement a solution that will best apply to the child. Alternatives to removal include providing access to family support services, or having the perpetrator leave the home instead of the child.

The new legislation has been met with mixed reaction. Some argue that there has been little improvement, that the definition remains both too broad and too narrow. Some professionals, including Judge Gove, suggest that the list of symptoms fails to capture all children who are in need of protection. Parents have their own set of concerns. All parents have bad days, and there is the worry that *any* act of commission or omission will immediately be labelled emotionally abusive. Berland reminds us, however, that the act has to be linked to an observable behaviour in the child. This, however, brings up another concern—some parents worry that they will be accused of emotional abuse if their child exhibits any of the behaviours listed, as these are also symptomatic of problems other than abuse. Berland stresses that the social worker's assessment will usually be backed by the advice of an expert and/or direct observation of the conduct. Further, the Ministry fully recognizes that the symptoms outlined may be linked to other causes. If a child is exhibiting these behaviours, the Ministry holds that *someone* should be taking a serious look at their potential cause and directing the child to appropriate help if no one else has intervened, whether or not emotional abuse is suspected.

At the very least, the new legislation provides a place to start. Berland emphasizes that B.C. has attempted to arrive at the best definition possible at this time, based on extensive consultation with the community, other jurisdictions, and the most up-to-date research. He is confident that the definition will continue to evolve as further advancements are made in the field.

Adoptive Parents: Coping With the Aftermath

While legislators and professionals continue to work towards a concrete definition of emotional abuse, adoptive parents are left to deal with the aftermath for children who were abused prior to placement. Dr. Pat Manly and I discussed coping strategies for parents who suspect their adoptive children have been exposed to emotional abuse. If children are showing some signs of emotional abuse outlined in the new legislation, parents should seek therapeutic help for the child, instead of taking it on alone.

Safety First

But therapy is just one part of the journey. Parents are faced with the fallout on a day to day basis. In general, children— like adults—learn more from experience than through instruction. Traumatized children, like all children, need clear expectations, consistent consequences, and a supportive, nurturing environment which promotes successful experiences.

The most important experience to create for children is that of physical and emotional safety. Being consistent creates a predictable world for the child so that he or she can begin to learn to trust. Consistency communicates trustworthiness in a fundamental way.

While the child's feelings need to be given a means of expression, they need to have safety containers so they don't have harmful effects. "So Johnny's angry. Johnny expresses his anger by kicking the walls down. That's not OK," Dr. Manly emphasizes. "And the child needs to learn that abuse is *not* OK. Ever." Early intervention with unsafe behaviour is essential.

The Child's Eye View of the World

Safety and trust are not immediately obvious to a child who has experienced trauma. Emotional safety may in fact feel *unsafe* to the emotionally abused child because it feels so unfamiliar. "If children have been exposed to a history of humiliation, this is the world they know. This is what feels like home to them. Anything else will feel fake. They might as well be on Mars. In their hearts, they believe they're garbage, so what's this new person talking about, *You're a terrific kid?!*—That's garbage, too. Everything they've learned about how life is doesn't apply here—so what are they going to do? The child may behave in a way that will be very challenging to the parents, as the child tries to get the parents to understand the world the way the world *really* is. The parents need to try to understand the child's world—and help the child come to understand the world around them."

Shame-based disciplinary approaches—and we're very much a shame-based culture—are particularly harmful to children who have experienced emotional abuse because shame gives them reinforcement that they really *are* garbage.

"It's important to be hard on the behaviour and soft on the child," Dr. Manly explains. "And it's not just nice language. When we're intervening, it's important to name the behaviour and define the problem behaviour as what's negative and needs changing. Because if we're defining the child as what needs to change, we're rejecting the child. And then we're reinforcing their view of the world—that the child is not valuable."

In other words, it's really important to be clear with children that what needs to change isn't characterological. "Do we ask children to be fake children, to please us? Many kids who've been exposed to abuse have learned how to do that very well in an attempt to control or modify an offender's behaviour. This is one of the difficult things about abuse—that children end up being in a position of assuming responsibility for someone else's behaviour."

Dealing With Feelings

It all comes back to treating each child with the particular kind of respect he or she needs—that doesn't mean treating them indulgently, but treating them with regard for who they are as they are, honouring where they come from, and accepting their feelings at face value. "It's often hard to do," Dr. Manly admits. "If a child says *I'm ugly*, it's human nature to say, *No you're not! You're a beautiful human being.* And then the child knows that they can't express their innermost, truest feelings to the person who is responsible for their care, and have their feelings understood." She gives an example of two adult friends having a conversation, where one is feeling very angry. "If the other person says to them, well, you're not *really* angry, it's even more infuriating. But it's easy to do this to kids without thinking."

It's important to acknowledge the child's feelings as they are. "Because the child feels that way, acknowledging the child's feelings doesn't mean that you agree or disagree with their view of the world—you're just acknowledging their feelings. You're just there to say, *Oh. I can see that for you, it really feels like that.*"

Adults often make the mistake of wanting to *fix* traumatized children. To a child, being "fixed" can feel like a rejection of their core self. "They don't want to be fixed. They want to be loved. They want to be understood. They want all the things that all kids want. They don't want to be changed—but with luck and persistence, they might be able to grow." The child, in most cases, has survived experiences that are probably foreign to the adoptive parents. Parents need to learn to accept that what happened in the past cannot be changed.

When children say astonishing things, like *I'm dopey, I'm no good, I'm garbage*, Dr. Manly encourages parents to use their perplexity to understand the child. "It's a mistake to use an adult experience of perplexity to deny what the child is experiencing and contradict it. If I feel ugly, and somebody says to me, *Really?! Tell me about that. I don't understand...* They're supporting me, making me feel like they really want to be there for me, *and* they don't get it that I'm ugly! For a child, if they're met with, *No, you're not! You're a beautiful person inside—* what are they going to do about that? They're stuck. As much as the parents want the child to be feeling differently, the act of trying to understand will make the child feel understood."

She cautions, however, that parents, have to pick their moment. "If it's time for the child to put away the toys, wash their hands and come to the dinner table, and the child chooses this moment to say, *I feel like garbage*, there may be something else on the agenda. It's OK to say, *We'll talk about that later, but right NOW it's time to clean up*. The whole challenge of parenting is to be really clear about your principal purpose in each moment when there are a million things going on."

Everyone's Feelings Count

While traumatized children need all the things that other children need, it's often harder to provide it for them because their behaviour can raise difficult emotions in the adults. "The first time that a three year-old child swears at you, it's astounding. The things kids may do or come up with can raise very difficult emotions in any caring heart." It is helpful for the adult to deal with those emotions by acknowledging, for example, that *When the child says these things, I feel FURY towards whoever it is who has done this to this child!* Or, *I just feel completely at sea*. But *this is MY feeling*, even though the child may be feeling something completely different. Acknowledging our own feelings and giving them a name can help make the feelings seem more manageable.

We need to give our own feelings the same acceptance and respect that we try to provide for others. "If we ignore our own feelings when we're dealing with kids, we're not going to be fully present for the children," says Dr. Manly. "And kids really need us to be present."

One of the things about good parenting is understanding that children are on a separate journey. While children can learn a lot and parents are able to assist with that, children have their own lives. What's difficult about parents' feelings is that they can be so strong and overwhelming at times. "What do you do about this fury—*who has done this to this child?!* How do you express that in a way that doesn't make the child feel that you're mad at them? You have to be really clear about that. It's a real dance. This whole thing of how we resolve our feelings is something that most of us do imperfectly. It's important to be forgiving of ourselves as well."

Reframing Success

We often tend to define success in terms of outcome or goal attainment—on the basis of things turning out the way we imagined they would. "Naturally enough," Dr. Manly explains, "this doesn't usually happen in the job of parenting. Children are full of surprises. Special needs children in particular can shine in some domains and have quite limited lifetime development in others. The successes of parenting are reaped in doing your job, so that this child has the best chance in the world."

She reminds us that ultimately, no one has direct control over anyone else's behaviour—after all, the parent's brain is not connected to the child's nervous system! Successful parenting involves the development and integration of a complex array of skills. The parent's task is to create the conditions where the child has the best chance for optimal development. The rest is up to the child.

Not A Sunday Jog

Parents must also remember to tend to their own self-care—they are no good to anyone if they are drowning themselves. Parenting at the best of times is a challenging undertaking. Parenting an emotionally abused child, like parenting any child with special needs, automatically puts parents into another league altogether.

Dr. Manly likes to think of it as the difference between an Olympic athlete and a Sunday jogger. Both the Olympic athlete and the Sunday jogger require some degree of skill, commitment, and a passion for running. However, the Olympic athlete makes training the focal point of his life and pushes himself to his limits, whereas it would be obsessive and dysfunctional for the Sunday jogger to do so. The Olympic athlete invests in the very best equipment, follows a strict diet, and trains even if it's raining... The Sunday jogger runs for recreation and pleasure, and hangs up his shoes to return to the office on Monday. Although the Sunday jogger may get sore muscles, the Olympic athlete has to be prepared to endure a lot of pain in order to make the team, because making it to Atlanta—or Sydney— is worth it. And like Donovan Bailey, who not only made it to Atlanta but sprinted his way to a gold—the Olympic athlete learns how to relax even in the face of the most gruelling pressure.

But we don't expect the Olympic athlete to make it to Atlanta alone. She needs a coach, a trainer, and a sport psychologist perhaps, to support her along the way. Likewise, adoptive parents of traumatized children need a support structure in place and the very best resources at their disposal, because it's certainly not going to be a Sunday jog. And not all athletes make it to Atlanta, Dr. Manly reminds us, in spite of training extremely hard. But every athlete strives for their personal best. "Athletes tell me that reaching a personal best is actually an incredible thrill," she says. And aiming for the Olympics is certainly a worthwhile goal.

References

Hart, S.N., Brassard, M.R., & Karlson, H.C. (1996). Psychological maltreatment. In Briere, J., et al. (Eds.), *The APSAC Handbook on Child Maltreatment* (pp. 72-89). Thousand Oaks, CA: SAGE publications.

Kadushin, A., & Martin, J.A. (1988). *Child Welfare Services* (4th ed). New York: Macmillan.

This article originally appeared in the SNAP newsletter, Vol. 12 #2, summer 1996. © 1996 Society of Special Needs Adoptive Parents

Trusting, A Challenge for Adoptive Families:
An Adoptive Parent's Perspective

by Tanis Doe

There are many experiences of parenting which causes hearts to pound with joy and fear. All parents experience anxiety over the health and well-being of their children and adoptive parents are no exception. Waiting the 9 months for a pregnancy to create a life can be stressful at the best of times and waiting years on an eligibility list can result in constant insecurity. Having a baby (or child) is one of the most significant changes in the lives of adults -- whether married, in committed relationships or as single adults, parents must learn to live with another "person" in an "immersion" environment. Sink or swim, sometimes with a life jacket, sometimes with lessons, but often with very little chance of hopping into a life raft. It is a long, hard struggle to learn how to be a "family." Adoptive families have the added benefit of *wanting* children, sometimes more than anything else, and the *wanting, waiting,* and *planning* can sometimes provide good therapy in terms of learning, reading and networking with other parents. Many parents, young or old, have to deal with the arrival of a child with very little preparation and it causes considerable upheaval in regular activities and routines.

Adoptive families may have waited several years before finally receiving a child for placement. At any age this child is a new member of the family and must be welcomed and involved with any current activities, but most often the activities do revolve around the new addition. Infants placed in adoptive homes often have only been in foster care or receiving homes after their hospitalization and may be able to bond quite well with their adoptive mother and father. There are several situations where even infants have difficulty bonding particularly if the very first months of their lives have been painful, traumatic or there is evidence of fetal drug addiction or alcohol effect. But, in many cases the bonding between adoptive parents and infants can happen successfully and lead to a mutually supportive relationship.

Adopting older children from 3 years to 16 years can bring great joys but also bring heartache. Most older children have been considered for adoption because their birth families are not able or willing to be parents. Sometimes the early lives of these adoptive children have been filled with violence, addiction and neglect. Both active abuse of children and passive neglect and lack of love will reduce the children's ability and willingness to bond with the new family. For many welcoming adoptive parents, this difficulty in bonding can be a very painful experience. I want to share some personal experiences to illustrate how the process of bonding, *trusting,* affects adoptive families.

My daughter was living in a school for the deaf when I met her. She was three years old at that time. It was almost two years before she finally immigrated to Canada and became my legally adopted daughter. I was very proud of our relationship and the fact that I had lived in her country of origin for a year and was familiar with her culture. I made special effort to reinforce her connection with her birth father and her racial/cultural identity. Although I had recently completed my MSW I had decided to continue my education and pursue a Ph.D. despite the economic consequences of being a student. I was able to locate a new community network in the new city after we moved but shortly after our move my daughter started developing behaviour problems.

At first they seemed to me indicative of a child wanting attention but later I became very worried. When I turned suddenly to talk to her (I use sign language) she would cower and shrink away. Sometimes when I checked on her late at night she was fully clothed lying on the floor instead of on her bed. My daughter disclosed sexual molestation by a neighbour (which happened in Canada) and during that investigation other stories emerged about her life prior to my adopting her. Because I was a trained social worker I followed all the procedures very closely in terms of police investigation and counselling after this disclosure but it did not reduce my anxiety about what had happened to her. Her behaviour and learning problems increased and we had several conflicts which led me to feel her rage or anger had increased. I still believe that we have "attached" and that our bonding was quite solid but she was still not able to fully trust me, and was quite willing to test me to my limits. Although she did not set fires, steal or bite other children, her behaviours were challenging to the point of feeling out of control. I loved her and was not willing to give up but there were days when I wondered if I had made a mistake in adopting her. I had not! She wanted me to give her up; she wanted me to prove that she was right in thinking no one would love her or keep her forever. Although her abuse was both physical and sexual, the most significant impact was "emotionally" and it still affects her ability to trust. I have worked with other children survivors of abuse and adults who have been sexually assaulted and it seems that no matter how well the body and outer self heals, the inner self remains scarred. For the loving adoptive parent it is very difficult to deal with apparent rejection, disobedience, defiance, withdrawal, and rage. For the child, however, this is what will protect them from pain of rejection, abuse and neglect. For the child who is learning to live with adoptive parents there *is no guarantee* of permanency. For an adopted child, outward displays of affection do not mean that there will always be love. For the adopted child there is always fear of abandonment for this is what the child has learned. Most children who are adopted after age 3 have experienced far more than many of us adults could imagine.

To most adoptive parents the new home should seem a castle and home of safety but to the child it is only one more building to keep them captive. I have to admit I felt that my daughter was being ungrateful at times when I compared her pre-adoptive situation to what I offered her, but now I know, in my heart, that she is not only thankful but is ready to trust me with her future. As a child who has experienced abuse from former caregivers and adults, it is very frustrating to be exposed to still more potential abusers without any reason to believe the abuse will stop.

Trusting — not only for the child who is adopted but for the parents who adopt — is the challenge for families. Adults must learn to trust in the healing power of children and children must learn to trust in the possibilities of love. Although there is far more awareness now about the effects of physical, sexual and psychological abuse on children, there is still social pressure to *not discuss it*. Adoptive families are often not given enough information about pre-adoptive history to know until years later the extent of abuse, and even later there is little chance of ever knowing the full truth. Attachment theories, counselling programs, treatment or therapy, can all contribute to the development of trust within adoptive families, but above all it takes *time*. Patience is required from all parents but especially crucial to adoptive parents of older children, and vital for those who have survived all forms of abuse.

Adult survivors of abuse and specialized therapists will tell you that abuse during childhood has long term effects on children *even* if there is no evidence of this in early childhood. Trauma has a way of resurfacing and it can do so at any time. Adolescence is a particularly vulnerable time for children, as they become adults, and it is also a time of blossoming sexuality and identity. Because of these stresses on a child, there is some likelihood that early trauma will in fact resurface and become a problem during these years. Some parents are better able to cope than others, and without some professional or peer support there are some disruptions where placements do not work, or children leave the adoptive home. I cannot imagine what would be worse, as an adoptive parent — having my child leave me voluntarily before adulthood, or being an adopted child needing to leave a family who has chosen me. I think that the challenges of the teenage years are especially difficult for the adoptive family.

However, these problems can also surface much earlier and many families have what we fondly call 20 year-olds in 5 year-old bodies. Many of the trust issues that are related to abuse and attachment can surface in younger children causing power battles and conflict to escalate far earlier than adolescence. There are very few studies which can accurately predict the effects of abuse on children because children are individuals. We must learn to treat them as such, and learn to trust, while they heal, and learn to trust us.

This article originally appeared in *Adoption Windows*, January 1994. It is reprinted here with permission of the author.

mental
health

IF YOUR CHILD DOES SUFFER
FROM A MENTAL ILLNESS, IT IS
IMPOSSIBLE TO IGNORE. THEIR
BEHAVIOURS AND MOOD
SWINGS AFFECT NOT ONLY HIM
OR HER, BUT ALSO THE WHOLE
FAMILY.
– Patty Burk

The Difficult Road Ahead:
Diagnosing Early Onset Bipolar Disorder
by Linda Duck

Lissa Cowan, SNAP's Senior Communications Coordinator, interviewed Linda Duck, a Canadian-Certified Family Educator, SNAP parent and long-time child advocate about the lengthy and difficult path to finding a diagnosis for her adopted son. Currently, Linda's son is receiving treatment in the United States for early onset bipolar disorder (EOBD) at a school that focuses on behaviour therapy. Linda notes in the interview that, with the right medication, (which sadly, isn't available in Canada yet), and a reward and consequence academic intervention program, he is finally thriving.

Lissa: We hear lots about bipolar disorder and the difficulty of arriving at a diagnosis. Why is this?

Linda: There's lots of medicine out there for depression and Attention Deficit Hyperactivity Disorder (ADHD) has been around for a long time and the public is aware of that. Ritalin and other stimulants have been around for 40-plus years and antidepressants have been around for longer than that. Both the doctors and the public see all those medicines and assume that there must be more cases of these disorders because there are more drugs available to treat them. There are far fewer mood stabilizers, anti-convulsant and anti-psychotic drugs on the market to treat bipolar disorder. Information on the brain is changing every heartbeat. Technology is changing before doctors can even get to see a workshop or read a book. Often advocating parents and families know more than the family doctors and psychiatrists they're dealing with. Also, the Internet has made lots of reputable information available to parents.

Lissa: Do you think the fact that more information is available for parents makes doctors more accountable? There are of course unprofessional websites that could make people misinformed about a certain illness.

Linda: Yes, well it's good to be aware of what sites are recognized and what ones aren't. NAMI, which is the National Alliance for the Mentally Ill, is the highest of the high.

Lissa: How old is your son?

Linda: He'll be 14 years old this summer.

Lissa: How long has he exhibited the behaviours that link to early onset bipolar disorder?

Linda: Since infancy.

Lissa: What was he diagnosed with having as an infant?

Linda: Reactive Attachment Disorder (RAD) and attachment. Well, of course, he's adopted but I've had him since birth and we carried him around and walked him using only a snugly. I was very aware of the importance of attachment and made our "attaching" a real priority. I went as far as to breast-feed him. The diagnosis of RAD was always referred to and we couldn't understand why or how that could happen.

Lissa: When did you first hear of the term early onset bipolar disorder in relation to your son? How old would he have been?

Linda: When he was in kindergarten he was referred to a mental health team because he just didn't do well. They told me I'd have to put him in special needs classes. Echoing through my mind was "What do you mean special needs?" That was the first time I'd ever seen him as having special needs. I just always thought, well, he's challenging and has attachment issues. I tried to make room for his personality without seeing him as difficult. In preschool he had separation anxiety. When I'd leave he'd curl up in a ball in the corner. He'd also have night terrors, an early symptom of bipolar disorder.

Lissa: At that time, did anybody ever use the term bipolar disorder?

Linda: No. Doctors talked about severe anxiety and separation anxiety and night terrors, but they were all separated out. I used to say it was like he was seizuring emotionally. He had tantrums, not unlike a typical two or three year old, only that his tantrums would go on and on. If I tried to use any form of discipline or a time-out, his horrible tantrums would escalate.

Lissa: Did you take him to see a psychiatrist?

Linda: No. Our family's paediatrician was our only medical professional. He never suggested a psychiatrist and I just thought if we needed one, he would refer us to one. I think he just thought our son was extremely difficult. I didn't see our son has being "mentally ill". He'd already been through a number of preschool environments and none of them could handle him. By the time he was in kindergarten we were referred to the mental health team. The man who oversaw the team was a psychiatrist who basically told me I was a bad parent. He gave me a pamphlet, which had guidelines that suggested what parents should do for time-out. If the child got out of the time-out chair, the parent was to say: "If you get out of that chair again I'm going to spank you."

Lissa: That's amazing. When was this thing printed?

Linda: 1996. It also said: "Clap your hands loudly in front of the child when you say the word spank." Another part of this document talked about restraining a child. What I never learned was that my son had a brain disorder (I like to refer to this as a neurobiological brain disorder) and restraining him only made it worse. I did this on occasion to keep him safe. I gave the team of professionals my twenty-two alternatives to spanking, ones I use in the parenting courses I offer. I figured that I had success with him and they didn't so I must know a thing or two.

I asked if he could be assessed and they told me that he didn't need to be. One time he came after me with scissors in the middle of the night. I think it was during a night terror or wake-up rage. By this point I'd done everything they said. I took everything away from him. He had nothing left in his room as he had destroyed everything he had.

Lissa: How old was he at this point?

Linda: Five years old. He was also talking in childlike ways about suicide, saying things like: "I want it to go dark," and "I want to bleed," and "I'm going to go live with hell." I thought to myself, I'm taking away everything and he has nothing to live for. I asked at the children's hospital if I could get him assessed and they kept saying no. I told the hospital that I'd fired my mental health team. The problem is, if they say you don't need a second opinion then you can't get one.

Lissa: It seems to take the power away from the parent.

Linda: Yes, it totally takes it away. So, I had to go in and take my file and say: "You're fired." Of course, they all looked at me like I was nuts. The children's hospital finally agreed to see my son. One of the psychiatrists at the mood disorder clinic said there was no hope for him, no cure, and that his brain was wired wrong. They told me that by the time he was entering puberty he'd either kill me, himself, or someone else.

Lissa: Do you know anything about the history of your child's birthparents?

Linda: No, not at all. Rule number one with a mood disorder is, you can't give a person with a mood disorder a stimulant or an anti-depressant. You must treat the mood disorder first and treat co-morbid (or co-existing) disorders second. They never treated my son's mood disorder, which made everything worse. That should have been a major clue for them as this is often the response to the wrong medication. Finally we put him on a mood disorder drug which worked but he gained a ton of weight.

Lissa: So that particular drug helped his moods?

Linda: Yes, it was Risperadol, one of the anti-psychotic drugs. Had we looked at mood disorder drugs first we would have been a lot further ahead.

Lissa: How many years would you say that the mood disorder wasn't being treated?

Linda: All of them but one. We never went back to that drug because of the weight gain. We went back to the anti-depressants and stimulants. So I got my old kid back. And he was so sick that he was cutting up frogs, starting fires, and making bombs. He was completely out of control.

Lissa: And now he's being treated in the US?

Linda: Yes. My family was falling apart. My daughter was on anti-depressants and there was no help for us. The funding for mental health support comes from the arm of the Ministry called Child Protection. So if you need funding to get your child into a treatment program it's not covered by your medical card. To get treatment for him from a therapist or any programs for mental health, it's not a health issue, it's a child protection issue. When I put him in a one-year treatment program, I had to sign him over to foster care. Doing this meant I lost my child tax credit and baby bonus. But that was the only way that we could get him funding for a program that was very useful.

Lissa: That makes little sense to me.

Linda: Well, the system sees mental health issues as being bad parenting, not medical. I don't get backup support because I'm a good parent. The program was designed for children like my son, but because the program was funded through the arm of the Ministry called Child Protection they kept denying me access. I went right to the top. I said I'd called BCTV and they were on their way with their cameras to pick me up. I told them that I was coming to their office to show them how I could become an abusive parent in order to get help for my son. Within 24 hours my son was in. But I had to lose all my rights as a parent to get my son into the program.

Lissa: How old was he at this point?

Linda: Grade Five. And he did so well in this treatment program. It wasn't like the public school system. It was focused on behaviour modification as well as academics. It was a program that was very much like the program he is in now down in the States. This was through the Children's Foundation. Most of the kids in the program were in foster care because other parents like me couldn't get the help. But it was hugely successful for my son. While he was there, we weaned him off the Risperadol and he began to fall apart again.

Lissa: Why did you wean him off this successful drug?

Linda: Because he gained so much weight. That was the horrible side effect of the drug. That said, now we have new and better drugs without this side effect.

For children, you have to find a cocktail of what works. There's rarely one drug that will work. Every child's different. So we went on with our pursuit. Bipolar disorder became one of the disorders we added to the list but it was never at the top. We never thought we needed to treat that first. Now we know that was a huge mistake.

Lissa: When you talk about early onset, what does that mean?

Linda: I found this information on the CABF website. The more we learn about the disorder the more prevalent it seems to be among children. It is suspected that a significant amount of children diagnosed with ADHD have early onset bipolar disorder. Or, have that as well as ADHD. According to the American Academy of Child and Adolescent Psychiatry, up to one third of the 3.4 million children with depression in the US may actually experience the early onset of bipolar disorder. In my practice I'm sure I see way more. We always thought bipolar was an adult thing.

Lissa: When you speak of "early onset" what do you mean? How early are we talking about?

Linda: Sometimes symptoms can arise as early as infancy. Bipolar disorder looks different in children. You can look at adults who have bipolar and a lot of them experienced these behaviours when they were young.

Lissa: When a child displays these behaviours, does that mean that he or she will have full-fledged bipolar disorder as an adult?

Linda: No, but I would not rule out the possibility. Bipolar disorder, like many, is a spectrum disorder. This means that in their lifetime when their brains settle down, given proper behaviour modification therapy through their growing and developing years, and paired with the right medicines they could live in a stable fashion for a while. Later, there might be a trauma such as death or the birth of a child, which could trigger a depression episode. But then they could live quite calmly having only residual shadow syndromes. It doesn't mean they'll be on lithium for the rest of their lives. Catch it early and you can re-pattern a brain. You can't cure it but if you get the right medicine that makes the learning possible and you get the right behaviour cognitive therapy the outcome could be infinitely better.

Lissa: But the success rate in terms of treatment, is higher if it's detected earlier.

Linda: Absolutely. It has a success rate of 85% plus if treated properly. Every time you give them the wrong medicine you hurt their brains. If they're not learning something positive about themselves they're learning something that's not positive. When caught later, the negative things that were learned have to be undone. I now have to teach a 13 year old that he's not a violent kid, that he can learn and is capable of love. He already sees himself as a write-off.

Lissa: What would you tell parents who suspect their child might have early onset bipolar disorder?

Linda: Go to the CABF and NAMI websites. Browse the parent and professional message boards and participate in on-line education seminars. Post a question in the "general discussion area". The top of the line experts will answer any questions you have. Find a reputable child and adolescent psychiatrist. The family doctors have less than 4% of their training on the brain so you can probably assume they won't treat a mood disorder. As I said before it's very important to treat the mood disorder first, not the depression or hyperactivity. Your baseline of success will go from there. The co-morbid (or coexisting) disorders need to be treated but this is secondary. Don't assume someone knows more than you do about your child. When something makes sense it's not more work because it empowers. Sometimes you need to go into places and find support networks because that's your salvation. You need to be an authority on your child. Don't settle for things you don't accept yourself.

This article originally appeared in the SNAP Newsmagazine, Vol. 19, # 2. © 2003 Society of Special Needs Adoptive Parents

A Fair Shake:
Tips on Parenting Children with Mental Health Issues
by Patty Burk

Of all the illnesses a child could have, mental illness seems to be the one most often under-diagnosed and also most misunderstood. It can place a great strain, not only on the immediate family members, but on the community in which the child interacts. Mental illness is an initially invisible disease that will externalize itself only upon further inspection. It has the ability to colour a child's world rosy and joyous one minute and dark and stormy the next. As a parent, there is a certain amount of pain in watching your child suffer through what should normally be a happy and carefree time. Only in recent years has more attention been paid to diagnosis and research on a variety of treatments for these troubled children. In many cases, little or nothing was done and more of a "wait and see" attitude was taken. It is estimated that one in five children suffer from an undiagnosed or untreated mental illness.[1]

Because of its relative invisibility, the signs of mental illness in children are often chalked up to "poor parenting techniques" (i.e. lack of consistency or limit-setting). Looking at symptoms and their intensity over a period of time can help differentiate between something temporary or something more serious that requires professional diagnosis and treatment.

Even More at Risk
Unfortunately, children who have joined their families through adoption are even more at risk because of poor prenatal care, prenatal alcohol or narcotics exposure, neglect, as well as multiple placements and attachment issues. If you have raised other children, you may have a good idea which behaviours are "usual" and which are not. If this is your first time parenting, do some reading and find someone with experience whom you can trust with confidentiality. Your family doctor is a good starting point. Document the behaviours you have concerns about and ask for a referral to a child psychiatrist, mental health or family counsellor. If you still have concerns and feel that they are not being met, approach the professionals again with documentation (written observations) in hand. It took well over a year for one family to be taken seriously by their paediatrician, who then apologized for the agony they had gone through trying to get help for their child.

If your child does suffer from a mental illness, it is impossible to ignore. Their behaviours and mood swings affect not only him or her, but also the whole family. Medications are now being used more successfully, and it can be positive to explore this avenue. As with all medications and diagnoses, it is advisable to get a second opinion, especially if you are feeling uncomfortable with the suggested treatment. Read up about the medications, paying special attention to the side effects. A scanty or absent medical history of your child may make the whole medical part a guessing game and it is always better to err on the side of caution.

Getting the Most from Respite Care
Don't try and brave it alone. Living with a child with mental illness is no less draining than living with an adult with mental illness. In some ways, it is more so because a child is less able to verbalize what he or she is experiencing. Respite, such as a weekend away, may suit your family fine, but also consider shorter stints. A couple of hours on a more consistent basis, (i.e. during an evening so you can sneak away to the movies or in the afternoon so you can have a nap) with an experienced caregiver can be very valuable. Knowing that you have a couple of hours to look forward to several days a week can sometimes keep you going.

Funds are available through post-adoption assistance to help pay for these breaks. If you feel you are not getting a fair shake, keep shaking that tree! I had to do this myself when explaining that $100 per month in respite wasn't quite enough for a stay-at-home mom of a mentally ill preschooler, while others with children in school all day were receiving five or six times that amount.

If you are lucky enough to have family members who understand your child's behaviours and you feel confident that your child will be well-supervised, approach them. Keep up with fresh air, exercise, sleep and vitamins (especially B). With the extra stress in your life, your body is probably deficient in this area.[2]

Keeping Ahead of the Learning Curve
Educate yourself and, to the best of your ability, educate others. If you have written material, you can provide it to the child's teachers, aides, counsellors and doctors, and other family members. Although, in the best interests of your child, be careful who you share with. Information should be shared on a need-to-know basis and the curiosity seekers who do not deal directly with your child don't fall into that category. The Internet as well as the SNAP library are invaluable sources of information on just about anything. Most professionals you visit will appreciate a well-informed parent; you may find the odd one who doesn't, but then maybe he or she is not a good match for your family. It's a learning curve for all and, really, who knows your child best?

Finding the Advocate in All of Us
Advocating is a word that strikes panic into the most reticent of us, and a righteous anger into those of us who are hot-headed. At its best, it simply means researching, knowing what rights your child is entitled to medically, educationally, and socially, and ensuring that his or her needs are met. Keep track of phone calls, letters, and meetings regarding your child. Remember to keep the avenues open. If one person is not able to help, don't berate them. Simply say, "I'm sorry that you're not able to help me out with this. Since we both care about my child, would you mind if I approached your supervisor?" Date your letters and don't wait for them to call you back. I once did this and the office worker called me back four months later!

Realize that regardless of your explanations, some people just aren't going to get it. Hold your head high. Who loves your child more than you? When the chips are down are these strangers going to be there to help you or your child? Make your decisions on what the best thing is for your child and family at the time. Try and take as pro-active a position as possible (for example, "if this happens, what then?"). In a lot of instances it only feels like there are 30 dozen sets of eyes on you as you walk your child firmly but lovingly back to the parking lot while he is screaming, "you're hurting me! I hate you!" If you need to, when you get a moment alone, you can sit down and have a cry. Forgive yourself; your children do. And know that you're doing the best you can.

A Different Path

Last summer, my son and I were walking back to the beach after a trip to one of the outhouses. There was a path, but my son chose instead to walk through the ditch, partway filled with water, brambles and rocks. I asked him why he didn't walk on the path with me; it was so much clearer and much easier to tread. He said, "no thanks, Mom. I want to go this way instead." Realize that as much as it hurts sometimes to see your children go down a certain road or make certain decisions, the decisions as they grow are ultimately theirs. You can consider yourself a successful parent if you have researched and taught them responsibility. Relax and enjoy the beauty of your child. Isn't your job as a parent to coach, not drive your child along the road of life and to ensure that you also enjoy the ride?

1 Attention Deficit Hyperactivity Disorder, Reactive Attachment Disorder, Oppositional Defiant Disorder, depression, etc. are all classified as mental illnesses. National Institute of Mental Health-Treatment of Children with Mental Disorders www.nimh.nih.gov.

2 Railey, Karen. How to Improve Fading Memory and Thinking Skills with Nutrition. chetday.com/vitamin_b_deficiencies.

This article originally appeared in the SNAP Newsmagazine, Vol. 19, # 2. © 2003 Society of Special Needs Adoptive Parents

institutions
& children

WE MUST REMEMBER THAT OUR
CHILDREN WERE "VICTIMS" AND
WE HAVE LEARNED THAT THERE
IS NO QUICK FIX OR MIRACLE
CURES—IT WILL TAKE TIME AND
PATIENCE AND PERSISTENCE
AND UNDERSTANDING.
— Parent Network for the
Post Institutionalized
Child

Post-Institutionalized Children & the Adoptive Family

by Lissa Cowan

Newspaper articles and TV news reports have probably taught many Canadians what they know about institutionalized children. From the searing portraits of children in orphanages in Ceaucesceu's Romania to hospitals in some African countries where children suffer from cholera and hepatitis A, diseases that, with adequate medication, are largely treatable. But media stories on the lives of these children are only part of the picture. What is missing is how these formative experiences affect the rest of their lives. What kinds of developmental, physiological, psychological and emotional scars are the children left with as a result of their traumatic entry into the world? And what happens when families adopt these children?

One Step at a Time

Much has been written in the area of developmental psychology on the importance of early stimulation of the infant from birth on. This typically takes the form of the caregiver holding, kissing, touching, talking, rocking, cooing, making faces, producing sounds with a rattle or musical toy, playing music and laughing. Without adequate interaction, sensitivity and stimulus on the part of the parent, the infant begins life without the necessary groundwork to build new experiences. This often means learning difficulties and complications relating to others later on. Inadequate personality development means an inability to give and receive tenderness, form friendships and adjust to new social situations.

Because children who have been institutionalized (especially older ones) are not used to lots of interaction and stimulus, it is important for the caregiver to take it slow the first little while. It's not a good idea to bombard the child with several toys at once, decorate the room with lavish colours and objects or invite family and friends over right away. Introducing people and things one step at a time will help the child not to be too overwhelmed. Eventually the child will be more accepting of his or her new environment. Many of these children have had multiple caregivers without the time to bond to one person. They might not have been able to complete the cycle of attachment. Having the prime caregiver spend lots of one-to-one time with the child at the beginning of the adoption will help everyone in the end.

Biology and Baby Neurons

Data from trauma literature suggests that on a biological level the central nervous system is affected by any overwhelming experience.[1] New research in developmental neurobiology has shown that the stimulation which the billions of neurons in the brain receive during early life has a major impact on their differentiation and function. The human brain is made up of cells (neurons). These cells form networks of connections so that every time the brain is stimulated new neuronal connections are being made. The more connections, the more neurons there are being integrated. This biological process plays a large role in forming the level of competence (our ability to learn) and coping skills of individuals as they grow up.[2]

For this reason it is important for new adoptive parents to obtain an immediate mental and neurodevelopmental assessment of the child. Knowing the child's speech and language delays, cognitive and intellectual, psychological and sensory-motor disabilities, will allow the family to plan the most suitable treatment strategies. For post-institutionalized 'infant early' toddlers, Developmental Neuropsychologist Dr. Ronald Federici suggests engaging in a variety of developmental play activities that include parent-child involvement. Toys that have different textures, colours, noises, music and movement are good tools for attaching the child to the caregiver and for learning.

Brief History of Institutionalized Studies

The phenomenon of institutionalization was being studied long before the term even existed. The well-known 19th century story of Kasper Hauser from Germany, who was raised in a dark room with little human contact, sparked the imagination of physicians, teachers and poets alike. Those who witnessed the man's behaviour noted his extreme reactions to people and things, along with a heightened sensitivity to his surroundings. Loud sounds made him cry; certain food smells caused vomiting. Unfortunately this story of abuse was not uncommon. By the 1940s and 50s a large body of work was being established around the topic of orphanages, foundling homes and nurseries. In his book *The Kaspar Hauser Syndrome*, Dr. John Money cites a paper titled "Personality distortion and early institutional care" (1940) by child psychiatrist Lawson G. Lowrey. Studying children who had been institutionalized from birth to 3-3 ½ years, he describes symptoms of hostile aggressiveness, temper tantrums, speech defects, shyness, sensitivity, stubbornness, sucking fingers, over-activity, sleep disturbances and more.

In a book published a year later called *Developmental Diagnosis*, Arnold Gesell and Catherine Amatruda comment on how a child's behaviours mirror his or her environments. Although today these ideas aren't new, at the time they were only just beginning to be explored. "Environmental impoverishment leads to behavioural impoverishment. It produces palpable reductions of behaviours. This is not to say that it produces mental deficiency; but it does produce symptomatic syndromes which are severe enough to make diagnosis difficult and to call for therapeutic intervention."[3]

The Process of Attachment and Bonding

Although the circumstances may differ, there continues to be reports today of children raised in isolation and deprived of human contact. Because of insecure attachment, normal child development is curtailed. Sometimes new adoptive parents are shocked when the child rejects their affections. Or sometimes the parents' affection is reciprocated but in a false, unreal way by the child. This is because their "preverbal and sensory motor experiences do not allow for maternal comfort and nurturing to be so readily accepted."[4] Research has shown that "sensory defensiveness"[5] is very common among post-institutionalized children who were not subjected to healthy child-rearing practices. Although the child may be defensive it is important for the caregiver to not "lose heart" and to continue to provide human contact and warmth.

Attachment is often described as a long-lasting psychological and emotional connectedness between human beings. When a child suffers trauma, be it through neglect or abuse, he or she has difficulty bonding or attaching to a caregiver. The normal development he or she must go through is impeded causing the child to develop a sense of mistrust, internalized rage and a need to control situations. In extreme cases, there have been known to be as many as 50 children for every worker in some orphanages and children's hospitals.[6] The chance of a child in these circumstances attaching to a caregiver early in life is small. Attaching helps the child to develop trusting relationships, most of all with his or her caregivers. If this is not done the child won't be able to form long-lasting relationships with others. Some therapies to assist the child in attaching to the caregiver include regressive therapy, behaviour management and re-parenting.

While attachment can be re-learned through therapy, bonding describes a relationship that simply exists and is irreplaceable. The term bonding refers to the unique relationship between a child and birth mother that occurs as a result of physical proximity during pregnancy and childbirth.

Family Histories

Institutionalized care studies show that the child who is available for adoption is most often from a single parent household with inadequate prenatal care and poor diet. Often these children suffer from malnutrition that could effect mental development. Fetal Alcohol Syndrome (FAS) is common amongst post-institutionalized children as are 'Failure to Thrive Syndrome', early infant-toddler restlessness, sleep, feeding disorders, and emotional/behavioural problems.[7] In other instances a child may be institutionalized due to parental rights being terminated, or, alternatively, the child might be removed from the family due to a serious illness or a physical or developmental disability.[8] Also, children who have major medical concerns or handicaps may be put into orphanages by their parents due to limited access to community support and services.

Institutionalization is often associated with other disorders such as Reactive Attachment Disorder, Attention Deficit Disorder, FAS/pFAS and Conduct Disorder. This is because often the child who has been institutionalized is the victim of neglect or abuse. It is said that over 50% of institutionalized children in Eastern Europe have low birth weights, were born prematurely or have been exposed to alcohol pre-natally. In the 1970s, psychologist Jean Ayres identified a neurological disorder called Sensory Integrative Dysfunction (SID). She concluded that children who are deprived of touch, movement, and sounds could exhibit SID. Some characteristics of the disorder are delays in speech and language, poor self-concept and over sensitivity to touch, sights, and sounds.[9]

It is often difficult for adoptive parents to understand what their adoptive child has lived through while in the institution. Because of this trauma during early development, the child may fall behind in fine and gross motor development, become defensive, cry constantly or revert to self-stimulation. It is important for parents to encourage healthy attachment even when it seems next to impossible.

Sources

[1]*International Adoption: Challenges and Opportunities*, PNPIC, Eds. Tepper, Hannon, Sandstrom, 4.

[2]Max Cynader, Ph.D., Fraser Mustard, M.D., *Early Intervention*, Child and Adolescent Behavior Letter, Brown University, Vol. 14, No. 7, July 1998.

[3]*The Post*, PNPIC Newsletter, Ed. Lois Hannon, Spring 1995, 2.

[4]Ronald S. Federici, Ph.D, *Raising the Post-Institutionalized Child: Risks, Challenges and Innovative Treatment*, 5, (See website: www. drfederici.com)

[5]S. Cermak and L. Daunhauer. *Sensory Processing in the Post-institutionalized Child*, The American Journal of Occupational Therapy, 1997, 51, 500-507.

[6]Federici.

[7]Federici.

[8]*International Adoption Challenges and Opportunities*, The Post, PNPIC Newsletter, Eds.Thais Tepper, Hannon, Sandstrom, 6.

9*The Post*, PNPIC Newsletter, Ed. Lois Hannon, Spring 1995, 3.
This article originally appeared in the SNAP newsmagazine, Vol. 18#2, March/April 2002. © 2002
Society of Special Needs Adoptive Parents

The Ultimate Tragedy:

"Institutional Autism": An Acquired Syndome

by Dr. Ronald S. Federici

When a child's memories of the few positive experiences of life gradually fade away, he or she may regress to the most infantile stage of development. In my visits to many Romanian institutions, I have observed children who have retreated into a fantasy world and have become extremely regressive in both their cognitive and psychological development. This regression can ultimately lead to a very infantile and autistic state in which the child exhibits an emotionally detached or preoccupied attitude. Being "cribbed" or totally secluded is the ultimate deprivation and isolative experience. Alone and scared. Scared and alone.

Children who "learn" to become autistic as a result of being institutionalized often have little, if any, language. They may be able to express five or ten words, but typically tend to grunt, moan, yell and shriek. Many tend to rock, sway and pick at themselves. These self-stimulating behaviors are the way they communicate and fill in the gaps of loneliness, boredom, and deep despair in their lives. Because these children have spent their formative years with other children who were similarly abandoned, it is understandable that they imitate the behavior around them. Eventually, these children regress to such low levels that they appear truly mentally deficient. For children who started out in life relatively normal, this is a tragedy.

This type of autism however, does not fall into any of the classic definitions of autism, Rett's Disorder, or even Childhood Disintegrative Disorder (although there is certainly "disintegration").

A unique and institutionally specific pattern of behaviors which constitute Institutional Autism often meet the following criteria:

1. Actual loss of physical height, weight and growth. Many of these children are not even represented on the growth charts or curves by which we estimate average growth. This is referred to as Psychosocial Dwarfism. The profound negative effects of malnutrition, untreated medical problems and social deprivation take their toll on the body and mind/cognitive development.

2. Does not look to be anywhere near actual age. In assessing many institutionalized children, I was unable to physically discern the actual age. This

is why, often, older children are assigned an age upon adoption, but are actually much older. Many of the girls have short hair and are dressed in boys clothing, making gender difficult to determine.

3. Loss of previously acquired language, or the use of language which is extremely regressive to the point that it resembles "infant babbling." This is commonly referred to as "institutional language." Along these lines, intellectual capabilities diminish to the point of pseudo-mental retardation with general cognitive skills difficult to measure.

4. Rapid deterioration of behavior to the point where the child exhibits primitive acting-out. This may include urinating and defecating on themselves and/or playing with urine and feces.

5. Illness, injury and starvation profoundly affect the body and brain development to the point that many children clearly develop a brain syndrome involving language deficits, attentional and concentrational problems, bizarre behaviors and deficient memory and learning.

6. Complete regressions to self-stimulating behaviors, such as rocking, head banging, hair pulling, picking at their own body, thrusting themselves into walls and windows, or enuresis and encopresis (playing with urine and feces). These severe behaviors imply that the child is trying to find a way to maintain internal physical and psychological "movements" which serve as a level of stimulation and as a way of passing the time. Rage, emotional outbursts, obsessive behaviors and self-stimulation may just be more ways to "keep busy" while also reminding themselves that they have no real identity or purpose in life.

7. The ultimate Institutional Autistic behavior is a complete regression to these self-stimulating behaviors as a way of filling in the gaps of loneliness, deprivation and despair. Over the course of time, if left to continually "practice" these behaviors, a child develops a repetitive pattern of newly learned movement, mannerisms and speech. The regression to the most self-absorbed and isolative way of life may be the "ultimate defense" in blocking out pain and suffering. Post-Traumatic Stress Disorder at its finest?

A better understanding of this unique and highly complex syndrome may help families approach the entire concept of international adoptions with more awareness. Many families are so anxious to adopt that they do not take the time or responsibility for learning about the complicated medical and psychological health issues before they adopt. So very often, many families finally reach qualified specialists after two or three years and multiple evaluations which have cost them thousands of dollars. By the time the proper diagnosis is made, families are often very angry and depressed. They tend to blame adoption agencies for misleading them and telling them their child did not have any significant cognitive and psychiatric/psychological problems and that "love would be enough." Love is an important intervention but it typically is not the recommended starting point for children coming from institutional backgrounds that do not understand the abstract concepts of human emotions. The word love needs to be "reframed" and used in a more helpful context which may be better termed "providing structure, safety and security."

The earlier the assessment and interventions, the better the outcome for the internationally adopted child. We know very well that children adopted out of the institution under the age of two years old stand a much better chance of rehabilitation or recovery. Our statistics for the older internationally adopted child indicated that approximately 75 percent may be deemed "high risk" for long-term developmental problems, with only approximately 25 percent appearing to be relatively unscathed or at least able to recover from institutionalization. This leaves a very large percentage of the "walking wounded" who are survivors but with a great deal of brain and emotional baggage. A strong brain and strong soul appear to be the critical factors in surviving an institutional life.

These statistics are, indeed, very concerning as the damaging effects of institutionalization are clearly seen impacting the medical and emotional growth of the child. Today, the new subspecialty of "adoption medicine" continues to provide valuable research, education and interventions for families pursuing international adoptions.

Unfortunately, severe diagnoses of autism, mental retardation, fetal alcohol syndrome/fetal alcohol effects or multiple learning disabilities will often persist until adulthood. It will take a very strong and dedicated family to help the child cope, work through these difficulties and find the proper adjustment and vocation. Therefore, before engaging in international adoptions, families must be well informed of all the risks and long-term effects of institutionalization. Children from institutional settings clearly need to be considered a "high risk population." No child who has been institutionalized will emerge unscathed. The younger the child (preferably under the age of 18-20 months) who can be removed from the institution via adoption will have a better opportunity of improving developmental delays at a more rapid pace, although the long-term effects of even short-term institutionalization will not clearly be evident until the child reaches school age years when learning aptitudes and abilities are assessed. It should be emphasized that, the lesser amount of deprivation will increase (but not guarantee) the chances of recovery or smooth sailing. There are no guarantees. Remember, life offers no guarantees, only challenges.

This article is excerpted from *Help for the Hopeless Child: A Guide for Families with Special Discussion for Assessing and Treating the Post Institutionalized Child,* (Dr. Ronald S. Federici & Associates, 1998). It is reprinted here with permission of the author.

Malnutrition & Its Effects

by Jennifer Lee

Those of you who have adopted children from international orphanages know how difficult it can be. Not only are you in another country with a whole other set of legal and medical procedures, but you are meeting your child for the first time, the child you may have seen in photographs and videos. You're emotionally charged and want everything to be perfect. More than anything, you want your child to love and trust you.

It is sometimes a shock to learn that your child has special needs and that these special needs might affect how she interacts with you. She might be unresponsive or frightened of you. She might be visibly ill or listless. And while many orphanages will provide you with some medical and family history, these may be incomplete or inaccurate. When you return home, it is often a struggle to get proper assessments. And the last thing you want to hear is that your child has been malnourished.

Malnutrition is a difficult and complex issue to deal with. Not only are its symptoms exacerbated by other environmental factors and disorders, but those very same disorders can mask the child's past of poor and inconsistent nutrition. We often hear about internationally adopted children who have developmental delays and difficulty forging relationships with their adoptive families, yet malnutrition as a possible cause for these challenges is rarely discussed. When a child from an institution has so many obstacles to jump over, nutrition history can sometimes be ignored.

It is common for children from institutions to be fed not when they are hungry, but on a schedule; a child in this situation may very well experience starvation pains until her assigned feeding time. And when she finally gets something to eat, it is the same bottle with the same liquid fed to her in exactly the same way as it was before. Is it any wonder, then, that a newly adopted child from an orphanage who suddenly finds herself in a new place with new caregivers will reject almost any food that is strange to her? Everything is scary and food is no exception.

Another common feeding challenge with post-institutionalized children is their tendency to hoard food and their attempts to eat unusually large amounts. Many of these children have had to fight for survival in their orphanages and literally scramble for food. While this may seem greedy or selfish, this is the behaviour that enabled the children to stay alive.

These kinds of behaviours are treatable and many parents find that if they provide nutritious meals and snacks, model good eating behaviours and do not force their children to change their eating habits suddenly and immediately, their children will gradually begin to display better eating habits. What is not so simple, however, are the physical and developmental results of malnutrition, which may have lasting effects on a child's life.

It is important to note that in many instances, it is almost impossible to say whether a child has a particular disorder because of malnutrition or because of environmental factors. As a child's symptoms are often mixed up together, it is important to look at all possibilities for treatment and to tell your doctors everything you know about your child and her background. In addition, many of the children in overseas orphanages have had poor prenatal care, which puts them at a further disadvantage and opens up the possibility of alcohol or drug related prenatal exposure.

In the beginning, a malnourished child may display a number of different characteristics including apathy, developmental delays (which can also be affected by experience and background) and atypical crying patterns. With good nutrition, most of these characteristics will disappear and children who may have been smaller than average will begin to catch up in their growth to the rest of their peer group. However, language and mental developmental delays continue to be problems and often manifest themselves as learning disorders and ADHD.

Children who have had poor nutrition in the most critical stages (prenatally to two years) often have difficulty with processing, applying and retaining information, all of which contribute to poor school performance. Although their physical growth can and often does catch up to their peers, the cognitive development can affect them for life, making school and work that much more difficult.

Food can play such a symbolic role in our lives; it is sustenance and comfort, an expression of love. When a child refuses to eat what you prepare or refuses to eat anything at all, it can seem like she is rejecting you as a parent. Keep in mind that food for the post-institutionalized child is not enjoyable and that her food behaviours have nothing to do with you and everything to do with her past. Show your child that food can be fun. Treating the results of malnutrition is not easy and many post-institutionalized children will have a complex combination of challenges to overcome, but there are good supports and services like SNAP available. Think about how far you've come already and you will be able to see how far you can go in the future.

This article originally appeared in the SNAP newsmagazine, Vol. 18#2, March/April 2002. © 2002 Society of Special Needs Adoptive Parents

Our Post-Institutionalized Children— Beyond Expectations:

An Adoptive Parent's Perspective

by Carol Fyfe-Wilson

My partner Don and I don't fit the usual profile of adoptive parents. At the time we adopted our gang, we were in our middle years and had survived the blending of five teenagers (my four and Don's one), a formidable task. You guessed it – either we were totally looney tunes or masochistic.

Shortly after we were married, we decided it would be great to have a child of our own, a little person our other children would love and share in common. Our children were in their early to late teens and a baby sister or brother was the last thing they wanted — silly us. The youngest requested we wait until he left home before the "replacements" arrived.

We chatted with friends who had adopted internationally and found out that children in both Haiti and Romania were in desperate need of families. We were told that the Haitian adoptions were being processed very quickly once a home study was completed and that the cost was very reasonable relative to other foreign adoptions. Little did we know!

We wrote a Haitian orphanage saying we would like to adopt two children under the age of three. We also stipulated there be no history of alcohol abuse or mental illness in their birth families. Shortly afterwards two darling little boys were proposed. Then the Haitian coup!! The process was delayed almost 18 months which increased the cost (monthly support for the children while they were still in Haiti) considerably. In the meantime, we heard of a little girl whose placement did not materialize so we were asked if we'd consider her. We were told she was four and had tuberculosis. Neither of these things were true.

It was April of 1992 and the children were now more than a year older. There was a brief pause in the civil war and planes were flying into Haiti whenever possible. We got passage on one, flew into Haiti, picked up the children and boarded another plane all within one hour. The information exchanged with the orphanage representatives did not include that the children suffered from neglect and malnutrition and had behavioural issues other than the fact that the youngest boy was somewhat hyper. There was an understatement!

The first inkling of behaviours related to their early lives occurred when our daughter refused to buckle up. My Creole instruction to her was too limited and it was simply ignored. She equally ignored instructions from the airline hostess.

Finally, the huge Haitian pilot marched down the aisle and spoke very firmly to her. Once airborne, the children settled in quite well except for the fact that Don had to frequently chase after Fraser as he was gleefully running up and down the aisles. It became evident when food was being served aboard the plane that the children had suffered starvation. C (our daughter) grabbed food off the trays as the attendant attempted to deliver the dinner to the other passengers. Spencer had a tantrum when C took something from his tray.

Once settled in our home, more behaviours linked with being institutionalized and their early childhood became evident. C and Fraser were very aggressive, Spencer whined and whined and all had frequent tantrums. C was defiant and seldom accepted my "no" without a battle, her emotions were extreme and Fraser's hyperactivity reached new heights. C apparently had suffered a disease related to malnutrition that left her blind in one eye. She bore a scar near her neck and was terrified the first time Don picked up a knife so we guessed she had experienced a very traumatic event. The children learned English and seemed to adapt very quickly to their new environment. The obvious signs of malnutrition disappeared, their parasites were dealt with and they grew by leaps and bounds.

It soon became very obvious that C was at least one and a half years older than we were told. This made her approximately six and a half to seven years old when she arrived in Canada. Conversely, Fraser was a year younger than indicated although tall for his age. We had two birth certificates for Spencer, the younger being more accurate.

Time slightly modified C's defiance of authority both at home and school. Structure, routine and authority were key, otherwise she and the boys seemed to get completely "out of control and off the wall." With the mastery of English, it became evident that C fabricated a great deal, sometimes for no apparent reason. She would often do what she was requested not to do despite consequences. She worked hard in school and did fairly well until abstract thought was required. Fortunately, most of her teachers were capable and experienced so elementary school was mostly a pleasant experience for her. Elementary children are generally more forgiving of the lying and manipulation so there was always a playmate. Logic seemed to escape her. Her hearing seemed to be selective (more than is typical of children) and her memory poor at times. She could not and does not maintain friendships for very long and she does not see the linkage between what she says and does to people being annoyed with her. She'd lock into an angry mood for days. As she entered puberty she became even more moody and preferred to play alone – or perhaps her friends were now less tolerant of the lying and her manipulations of them.

Over the years, I sought help with her inappropriate behaviours but because she can verbally present so well, I was ignored or told her behaviour was typical. I had had four other children and I knew what was typical and she certainly was not. In all fairness I must say we lived in very small cities where professionals were not experienced with children adopted from developing countries and the consequences of malnutrition or early childhood trauma.

Spencer, although nearly a perfect child with excellent social skills, had speech and language difficulties. Fraser continued to be hyperactive and volatile with minimal social skills. He was also very intelligent. In an attempt to slow him down and curb his outbursts, I sought to modify his diet which was already very nutritious and balanced. I contacted the nutritionist at the hospital and was eventually led to a paper on the neurological impact of malnutrition. A light goes on! I soon became aware of FAS/E and strongly suspected it to be a major contributor to C's development. Eventually I was referred to papers on the neurological impact of early childhood trauma such as neglect and violence from living in a war zone to family violence.

At 14, C was told by her friend that she could get a foster home that would allow her to do as she pleased, with no rules, no expectations and no structure. She believed this friend and could not be dissuaded by any evidence to the contrary. When I literally stood in her way, she became violent and broke free. It took two large RCMP officers to capture her. She was placed in foster care. Within a week she apparently had forgotten why she was in care and began to fabricate stories about us and tried to manipulate social workers, foster parents and the school principal. The social workers admitted they had never encountered a child like C before. Her first foster placement was disastrous for they were giving her a "taste of freedom" that we supposedly did not. Within three months, the foster mother had become ill due to the stress, the foster father was totally exasperated and C was spiralling out of control. I had written the Minister of Children and Families and mentioned that her behaviour had deteriorated drastically and that she needed structure, routine, more supervision than usual and clear expectations. The Ministry had labelled her with Reactive Attachment Disorder but I insisted that she also suffered from neurological disorders due to malnutrition, early childhood trauma, neglect and possibly FAS. Currently C is in a small, specialized group home that is very structured and routine with clear boundaries and expectations. The foster parent is supportive of getting appropriate diagnosis of C so that supports can be put in place. She now agrees with me that C has all the symptoms of FAS/E and is following her suspicions up by keeping the appointments with a psychiatrist that I *insisted* the Ministry make for C.

Even though we were experienced parents we were not prepared for the behaviours exhibited by our adopted children and had to plan alternative parenting strategies. We had to be very clear about the issue at hand as two of the children tended to manipulate in attempts to avoid or distract us from the issue, or they simply did not understand until requests were reiterated a number of times. As the boys were younger when we brought them home, they hadn't buried their past experiences and we found that if we encouraged them, they could express what had triggered a certain reaction. For example, Spencer was taking all the ice cream even though others hadn't had their share. Don made Spencer put some back. Spencer just flew out of the house. I went after him and with some gentle prodding he said, "I remember people taking my food and I was hungry." Some of Fraser's "wig outs" were triggered by his having feared for his life.

Since C has left home, we are much more relaxed and Fraser stopped bedwetting almost immediately. Spencer blossomed. I was able to get Spencer an appointment with a paediatrician because of his continued problems with speech and language. He was diagnosed with ADD. Fraser continued to become more unmanageable at home and school but because he is bright and charming, the two general practitioners I saw would not refer him to a paediatrician. I spoke to Spencer's paediatrician about Fraser and he was subsequently diagnosed with ADHD (well, no kidding!!). Both boys are now on Ritalin and doing ever so much better.

With family support and the help of a dear friend who is a psychologist, we were able to get through the devastation of having our daughter leave home under such terrible circumstances. We have come to accept that she will spend her growing up years in care and that she probably will not be able to live independent of support or supervision. With proper supports, she will lead a productive life rather than one on the streets. Making sense of C's behaviours and trying to understand and reason with her consumed a lot of time and energy. Now I have come to accept that often what she said or did made sense only in her mind and maybe for only that moment. That's just the way it is.

Dear Verna, the SNAP librarian, sent me numerous books in my quest for knowledge and understanding. Among them was *Can This Child Be Saved*. There we were, described in the first couple of chapters. This told us that we were not alone in our experience. This offered immense relief for the guilt we felt for having "failed" as parents. I highly recommend this book to all adoptive parents.

This article originally appeared in the SNAP newsmagazine, Vol. 18#2, March/April 2002. © 2002 Society of Special Needs Adoptive Parents

transition to adulthood

TODAY HE IS NEARLY NINETEEN
AND HE STILL NEEDS A SAFETY
NET (HIS MOM) AND HE STILL
NEEDS A SOUNDING BOARD
(HIS MOM) AND HE STILL NEEDS
HELP WITH HOMEWORK (FROM
MOM).

– Leon's mom

Growing Up:

The Transition to Adulthood for
Young People with Special Needs

by Sara Graefe

You can't stop the clock. It's just one of those things: children grow up, special needs or not. Transition periods are typically hard, as both children and their parents adjust to growth, change and new developmental tasks. Further, some special needs conditions such as FAS make it particularly difficult for those affected to deal well with change. You might remember—or be currently coping with—the passage from infancy to pre-school, pre-school to school years, or the pre-teens to adolescence. However, the transition from adolescence to adulthood has been noted as one of the most stressful times for many so-called "typical" families. It is not surprising, then, that studies have found this period to be especially stressful for parents whose older children have disabilities (Ferguson, Ferguson, & Jones, 1988; McDonald, McKie, Newton, Webber, & Steele, 1992; Mellon, Wilgosh, McDonald, & Baine, 1994).

"Making It"

Most parents worry about their adult children "making it" independently in the world. Mainstream media portrays parents dealing with "empty nest syndrome," working through grief, loss, and letting go, while at the same time celebrating their child's passage into the adult world. But "growing up" can mean different things. A person with special needs may reach age of majority in chronological years, but emotional, intellectual and/or physical functioning may remain at a child or adolescent level.

Parents' worries about their adult children "making it" thus take on new dimensions when special needs are involved. In many cases, the young adult with special needs simply *won't* make it on his/her own without appropriate services and supports—after all, such interventions throughout childhood and adolescence may well have helped you and your child get this far to begin with. And unfortunately, fighting for services doesn't get any easier once your child has grown up. In fact, many young adults "hit the wall," a term coined by the B.C. Coalition for Community Service Provision for People with Disabilities, meaning that crucial supports are often only available until their 19th birthday, leaving them suddenly high and dry. This is coupled with the need for additional services, such as appropriate vocational and housing options. Parents are forced to navigate "confusing and often fragmented" (Emerson & Moon, 1987) adult service delivery systems for the first time.

You may face additional concerns over issues such as sexuality, behavioural problems, social skills and emotional stability of the young adult with special needs. And you may find yourself wrestling with your very own, specific grief, because your child's passage to adulthood isn't the one society has prepared us all to expect—your child may not be headed for university or marriage, for example, and you have to realign your expectations, even expectations you didn't know you had.

Or quite simply, as Duncan SNAP parent Ro de Bree puts it, you might be grieving the fact that there is not going to be an emptying of the nest in "standard fashion." Perhaps your young person will stay in your care for years into adulthood, due to their physical care needs and lack of appropriate alternatives. On the flip side, your youth may leave home sooner than anticipated, not always under the most desirable circumstances—running away, living on the street, or moving into custody of the criminal justice system. Finally, as children with special needs grow up, parents are increasingly faced with the question that is uncomfortable enough to contemplate, let alone talk about—*what will happen to my child when I grow old and die?*

Plan Ahead
Simply thinking about these issues is enough to cause stress, anxiety, grief, and general discomfort. It is not surprising, then, that many parents avoid dealing with these questions until they find themselves in the throes of transition. The Planned Lifetime Advocacy Network (PLAN) is a British Columbia-based organization committed to assisting families create a secure future for their children with disabilities. According to PLAN, the main thing that holds so many people back from preparing for this transition is *fear*—be it the fear of opening up and discussing intensely personal and private matters with others, the fear of death, or the fear of making a mistake, of not being perfect (which is ironic, given that in trying to make perfect decisions, we risk indefinite delay.) Further, as B.C. educator Chris Horrocks notes, most parents are so overwhelmed from meeting their child's day-to-day needs that they have no energy left to even *consider* next week,

let alone the future.

However, planning ahead is key, both to reduce your own stress and to ensure that the transition goes as smoothly as possible for your young adult with special needs. Even though this means investing your time and energy *now*, while grappling with fear and other uncomfortable issues, you and your child will be better prepared to face the unknown.

SNAP parent Chris Primus of MacKenzie agrees. She has two adopted children with FAS, one twelve, the other seventeen, and wishes she had known this early enough to intervene sooner with her seventeen year old, who has started to experience the bumps and grinds of transition. Being in a small, northern town with few resources, she has had to learn from trial and error. "Start teaching life skills as soon as possible," she emphasizes. "The earlier the intervention, the better." While she worries about the future of her older teen and hopes that current interventions aren't too late, Chris' hard-earned experience has enabled her to put appropriate strategies in place to start preparing her twelve-year old for adulthood *now*, seven years shy of legal majority. Learning hands-on within an individually-tailored work experience program, this pre-teen has already experienced success with life skills and holding down a job.

What Planning Ahead Looks Like...

Planning ahead can involve a whole range of things. It can start with something as simple as exploring what kinds of services, employment programs and residential options are available for adults with your child's specific needs. If there's not much out there, you have lots of lead time to consider alternatives, fill in the gaps, strategize with professionals currently involved with your child, and lobby for improved services. In Chris Primus' case, she responded to the lack of services in small town MacKenzie by helping form the Life Skills Society, a new agency which helps people with special needs prepare for community living from an early age: "Sometimes, especially in a small community, you have to get something going yourself." She encourages parents to look at what other communities are trying—the Life Skills Society, she says, was an "idea from someone else's idea."

Planning ahead can also mean building on the child's personal strengths at home from an early age. Teaching social and living skills, cultivating personal interests, and bolstering self-esteem can better prepare many young people with disabilities for adult living than a focus on academics and school work. In the case of individuals affected by FAS, for example, Dr. Ann Streissguth of the University of Washington (1997) notes that "the real goal is a healthy emotional life... Some of the most important things a child with FAS/FAE can be taught at home to prepare for life after school are: to be a friend and to behave in a socially appropriate manner; to be alone and to find constructive, solitary things to do; to work and enjoy working"(p.190). Streissguth emphasizes the importance of a cohesive, supportive family to give children with disabilities something exciting to belong to and talk about, as well as extracurricular venues of success, to help compensate for low academic achievement or peer group rebuffs that might otherwise lead to depression or dependence on an undesirable peer group: "A medal in the Special Olympics," she notes, "can go a long way toward offsetting difficulties with multiplication tables"(p. 193).

Be Creative

Some young people benefit greatly from life skills and vocational training that is available to them through the school system. However, such programs have proven less successful to others because of their failure to meet specific needs. An employment training program broadly labelled "for individuals with mental disabilities," for example, may cater to the needs of individuals with Down Syndrome, but not take into account the different characteristics and needs of a young person with FAS. Also, in smaller communities, there's bound to be less choice. In MacKenzie, the only opportunity for learning life skills in the school system is through Home Economics class. "And taking lots of Home Ec. just doesn't work for a lot of these kids," Chris Primus reminds us.

The alternative? "Be creative," she stresses. The Life Skill Society is but one example of a creative solution. The Primus family is also helping their twelve-year old son with FAS prepare for a career in vending. He currently has a job refilling pop machines, something he loves and does competently. This whole thing started while he was still attending school and needed time out from the regular classroom due to behavioural needs. He would regularly assist the janitor in filling the school pop machines, collecting the money, and so on, following the same predictable steps each time. As a reward for successfully completing the task, he got to choose a free pop or juice each week. When his behavioural problems worsened and he was forced to withdraw from school, one of the things he missed most was "his job." It was this that spurred the Primuses to find a way for their son to continue "his job" in the outside community—"We had a mission—to hunt down more pop machines!" Chris laughs. He currently fills a number of vending machines around MacKenzie, his reinforcement now being money as opposed to a free pop. "The key to it all," Chris reminds us, "is accepting who they are and what they *can* do—instead of who they aren't and what they can't."

Personal Future Plan

Planning ahead can also entail drafting a life plan for your child with special needs, or as PLAN calls it, "creating a secure future" for your adult child which will continue to exist after you and your partner pass on. PLAN's book *Safe and Secure: Six Steps to Creating a Personal Future Plan for People With Disabilities* is an excellent guide with hands-on exercises to help parents craft a custom-made plan for their own loved one. The book covers diverse ground, from clarifying your personal vision of the future, building a web of supportive relationships for your child, housing issues and solutions, preparing for decision making, developing your own will and estate plan, and finally securing your Personal Future Plan by appointing a monitor (e.g. individuals or an organization such as PLAN). A copy of this resource is available from the SNAP library, or parents may purchase their own copy directly from PLAN *(a good idea if you want to take full advantage of the interactive workbook exercises!).*

PLAN also publishes a quarterly newsletter for its membership and offers numerous direct services, such as assistance with will and estate planning, information and referral on all future planning issues, workshops, family meetings, and help in developing Personal Networks of support. Interested families can become members by paying the one time initial Lifetime Membership contribution of $1000.00 (tax deductible). An instalment plan is available. *(For more information, contact Planned Lifetime Advocacy Network, 260-3665 Kingsway, Vancouver, BC, V5R 5W2, www.plan.ca. Phone (604) 439-9566 or toll free 1-888-696-PLAN)*

On Guardianship

Parents of young adults with disabilities are often concerned about their child's ability to make decisions. Mental retardation, cognitive impairment, impulsivity, inability to understand cause and effect, and mental illness are just some examples of special needs conditions that would impact decision-making capability. As a mother of a young woman with a dual diagnosis complained at a recent "Through the Lifespan" conference, "My daughter's legal rights are going to kill her!" (Warner, 1996).

Some parents believe that the only way to keep their child safe is to have complete control over all their decisions—to remove their child's legal rights as an adult and secure legal guardianship. However, this is a very intrusive and costly solution which will strip your child of not only any power, but also all citizenship rights. In the eyes of the law, your child will no longer be a person. PLAN and other family advocacy agencies have long been pressing for alternatives to guardianship, wherein the family is involved but the person with special needs retains their rights as an individual—i.e. representation agreements and joint decision making which allow people with disabilities to choose one or more people to assist or make decisions about their health and personal care as well as their legal and financial affairs.

As Al Etmanski notes in PLAN's *Safe and Secure,* "By now it should come as no surprise that we believe the only real protection for those you love is the people who know them and are in a relationship with them. In other words, it's the relationships that count. We look at relationships as the first resort and guardianship as the last resort"(p.88). *Safe and Secure* proposes some helpful strategies and alternatives to guardianship for parents planning for the future.

Search and Reunion Issues

For adopted people, identity issues in adolescence and young adulthood may kindle a desire to search for their birth parents, to gain a clearer sense of themselves. If your child was adopted under the closed system in British Columbia (prior to November 4, 1996), they and their birth parents will be able to obtain identifying information about each other once the child turns nineteen, except where a disclosure veto has been filed. At age of majority, only your child and the birth parents have the authority to file a disclosure veto or no-contact declaration.

Adopted parents of a child with special needs may be understandably concerned with their young adult's ability to cope with the reunion process. You may have fears about your child's health and safety due to their special needs and/or history with the birth parents. These concerns are real and need to be acknowledged. However, under the current *Adoption Act,* greater openness is encouraged and more opportunities for reunion will occur, so it's best to be prepared ahead of time. Begin to deal with the possibility of reunion now rather than later, and take pro-active steps to support your child.

Letting Go

Once you've confronted your fears and feelings around your child's transition to adulthood, and have done your best to put plans and early interventions in place, you ultimately have to let go. Let it be. After all, you can't stop the clock. Your child will grow up. No matter how much you've planned ahead, the transition time itself will probably feel pretty stressful, although hopefully less overwhelming and bleak than it once seemed. Letting go doesn't mean you can't revisit and revise your plans as needed. The trick is to keep rolling with the punches—something you're probably good at by now, having raised a child with special needs.

And if you're faced with what seems like the worst case scenario—your interventions haven't been successful or have come too late—this doesn't mean you've failed as a parent. As psychologist and fellow adoptive parent Brenda Knight reminds us, "We're not there to make a person's life; we're there to be with them while they live it. There are some people in the world who may not make it. And there are some people who will. We can help them, we can hold their hand, and we can support them, but there are some things we cannot control.... Being a parent means that you're an advocate, and you're somebody sending them love from somewhere in the world... making sure that the child gets services, and providing the child a place to phone home to.... You haven't wasted your energy and love, because the children will know what a family is, and what good people are. They will be carrying that with them for the rest of their life...."

This article originally appeared in the SNAP newsletter, Vol. 13 #4, winter 1998. © 1998 Society of Special Needs Adoptive Parents

A Family PLAN for People with Disabilities
by Al Etmanski & Vickie Cammack

For the first time in history, people with serious disabilities are outliving their parents. Advances in medical technology, improved health care availability, higher social expectations and community living have ensured a longer life for our friends and family members with disabilities.

Our 23-year-old daughter Liz is a good example. Before she was five she had two life-saving operations that would have been too risky just a few years earlier. Nowadays, people with Down syndrome are living on average into their sixties. Compare this with a life expectancy of nine in the 1920s and thirty in the 1960s. There is no reason to believe Liz will not live as long as her siblings.

In the next decade, close to six million families in North America will be caring for an aging relative with a disability. The immensity of this fact is slowly creeping into the consciousness of the disability community and will soon command the attention of government policy-makers and even the corporate sector.

This demographic trend, however, underscores a worry that perches on the shoulders of every parent from the moment we discover that our child has a disability. Although thinking about the future is a natural extension of being a parent, those of us who have a child with a disability must think not only about our own lifetime but also their lifetime. As one parent in Ottawa recently commented, "I need a 'drop-dead' plan." While we all know death is not optional, we tend to ignore the fact that we ourselves will die and that we have no way of knowing how long we'll be around to care for our children.

As more and more Canadians reach their senior years, pressure is exerted on society's systems and institutions to respond. This in turn has the benefit of raising awareness of the importance of planning for the future of our sons and daughters with disabilities, regardless of their age—or our age, for that matter.

Creative Responses Emerge

Fortunately, many families across Canada are developing creative responses to what some people have described as "aging anxiety." And the solutions are emerging from the age group one might expect: parents who, now in their senior years, are having to confront their own mortality. These men and women, many of whom were leaders in the community-based disability movement that emerged after the Second World War, are not content to just resolve their own future planning challenges. They are also passionate about sharing their pioneering efforts with younger families.

We work for one such group: the Vancouver-based non-profit charity, Planned Lifetime Advocacy Network (PLAN). In 1989 a group made up of fifteen families came together to help each other answer the stark question, "What will happen to our sons and daughters with disabilities when we die?" These parents, whose average age was seventy, created an organization to be a container for their worries, dreams and solutions.

Today, John Ralston Saul is our National Patron and, thanks to the J.W. McConnell Family Foundation and the Vancouver Foundation, PLAN is a national organization with affiliates from coast to coast. It is also inspiring international collaboration with groups of families in the United Kingdom, Australia, New Zealand and throughout the United States.

Planning a Good Life

For far too many people with disabilities, life means being surrounded by paid professionals and support workers. At PLAN we like to think about the future by focusing on what constitutes "a good life." Instead of asking "What programs or services does your son or daughter need?", we ask "What would be a good life for your son or daughter?" The responses are rich, unique, often poetic and even spiritual. In general, families' views of a good life for their family member with a disability include:
- having caring loving relationships;
- living in a place of their own;

- making a contribution to their community;
- having authentic choices; and
- enjoying basic financial security.

Families believe programs and services should supplement, not supplant, a good life.

To help families create a good life for their family member with a disability, PLAN offers these supports and services either free or for a reasonable fee:

Consulting on Future Planning

Through a quarterly newsletter, a national magazine, workshops, seminars, peer support and on-line consultation, we provide up-to-date information on:
- will and estate planning;
- discretionary trusts;
- government benefits;
- tax benefits;
- home ownership for the individual with a disability;
- alternatives to guardianship; and
- a seven-step process to complete a Personal Future Plan for a person with a disability.

Creating a Personal Network

To be isolated is an enormous tragedy and, as Mother Teresa observed, "a most terrible poverty." Loneliness may already be the most significant handicap experienced by our family members with disabilities, and their loneliness may become even more of a threat after we are gone.

To reduce this isolation and loneliness, PLAN facilitates the development of a Personal Network for people with disabilities. We have discovered that, not only is it important for them to be in relationship with several people, but it is also important for each person in the network to be connected to each other. In this way, a Personal Network truly creates ties that bind. We have also learned that everyone, regardless of age or disability, can be welcomed into friendship. This has become an important source of hope and inspiration for aging parents as they watch the members of their son's or daughter's Personal Network becoming their eyes and ears, arms and legs.

Committing for a Lifetime

The ultimate support we offer families is a Lifetime Membership. We commit as families ourselves to oversee, monitor and ensure the well-being of members with disabilities when their parents become infirm or die. This commitment is bolstered by a protective covenant ensuring families will always be in control of the organization. PLAN's commitment to its members is also protected by our financial self-sufficiency; we have no ongoing reliance on government or corporate funding. PLAN is, in effect, the parent- based backup to the plans that each family makes.

Supporting Younger Families

PLAN has evolved from its initial appeal to older families so that we now also support families with young children. A particular joy is our "Spinoza the Bear" program which provides each child with a talking teddy bear and their families with a PLAN membership and connection to other families dealing with the same challenges.

"Hands-on" practical advice and support to families have always been the nuts and bolts of what we do at PLAN. Over the years, however, we have come to realize that we also offer something equally important, though less visible: inspiration. The most vital consideration for all of us is not how long we will live but how well we will live. Planning for the future is the best excuse for changing the present—both for the individual with a disability and for their family members.

This article originally appeared in *Transition*, a publication of the Vanier Institute of the Family, Spring 2002. It is reprinted here with the permission of the Planned Lifetime Advocacy Network. For further information about PLAN, contact 260-3665 Kingsway, Vancouver, BC, V5R 5W2. Phone: 604-439-9566, email: inquiries@plan.ca, web: www.plan.ca.

The So-Called "Empty Nest":
An Adoptive Parent's Perspective

by Ro de Bree

It's not as if I had no warnings. My alcohol affected children hadn't managed kindergarten, or Cubs, or after school jobs, or peer relationships with grace or finesse, so why would their official departure from home be any different? Why would there be any expectations of the nest emptying in standard fashion? Why would I even contemplate "normal" from this family?

We had a stretch of seven years between the arrival of our oldest, fifteen pounds at three, but never designated "special needs," and the arrival of our youngest, twenty months of spitting temper. Five of them altogether, with an eight year span between either end. I thought their going would take as much time as their coming, but it didn't; in eighteen months we had completed four painful departures out of five.

Dreams of eventually living ordinary, useful adult lives—for all of us, not just the children—were always there. But in the times when my expectations were starting to destroy me, and my only hope was—and is—for changes within governmental systems, those dreams and hopes were a safety valve too, a temporary protection from reality.

Reality can be harsh, especially for those of us whose immature, adopted children leave home years too early, and quickly become members of the youth criminal sub-culture. Close friends, and even other family members, sometimes have great difficulty understanding and accepting our attitudes—"My child; right or wrong." The tremendous need for emotional support while my son was an active participant within the Criminal Justice System, and the value of the SNAP group, who upheld me while I advocated for him, can never be overemphasized.

Older couples, whose adult children must return home after a cheerful and positive leave-taking, at least expect to welcome back a more mature adult. But we often face an even trickier problem: grown F.A.S. children who don't understand that they are supposed to leave. And my returnees, who process information so poorly, and who bring all the negatives of their last institution trailing along behind them, expect everything connected with Mom and Dad and home to have remained exactly the same.

During the whole of their lives, these FAS young people have offered broad challenges; for me, the most difficult challenge to meet has been the constant lowering of expectations. Their lifestyles, their morals, and their ethics will never be my choices, and my standards are no longer theirs.

But through these same young people, my understanding has also widened, particularly in the area of preserving and maintaining caring relationships. The bottom line—it is only given to us to move through life graciously and lovingly, ourselves; it is not given to us to control others. In the end, each of us has to make her own journey, and mine, although not always easy, has taught me one of life's most valuable lessons—to replace expectations with acceptance.

This article originally appeared in the SNAP newsletter, Vol. 13 #4, winter 1998. © 1998 Society of Special Needs Adoptive Parents

some parting words

Hang In There

You've already demonstrated your commitment to your child and to yourself by making it this far—by weathering the struggles of parenting a child with special needs, hanging in there no matter how much your child has tested or challenged you, and even just by picking up this book. It's probably been hard, but you've made it this far. Keep on hanging in there the best you can, and don't forget to take care of yourself.

Even if you're faced with what seems like the worst case scenario—the interventions have failed or come too late, the child has left home or the child has been removed from the home—this doesn't mean you've failed as a parent. It is helpful to remember that you're not there to make a person's life—you're there to be with them while they live it. You can help them, hold their hand and support them, but there are some things you cannot control. As Brenda Knight points out (page 155, *A Toolkit for Parents*), being a parent doesn't mean you have to live with the child twenty-four hours a day. Being a parent means being an advocate, somebody sending that child love from somewhere in the world, making sure that the child gets services, and providing a safe place for the child to phone home to. In some circumstances, parenting from a distance is the best way of taking care of yourself and taking care of your child.

resources

Print, Audio & Video Resources

Complete Adoption: Everything You Need to Know to Adopt a Child (2000) Laura Beauvais Godwin and Raymond Godwin.

The Encyclopedia of Adoption (1991) Christine Adamec and William L. Pierce

INVISIBLE DISABILITIES

Educational Care, a System for Understanding and Helping Children with Learning Differences at Home and in School (2002) Mel Levine, MD

FETAL ALCOHOL SYNDROME

Living with FASD: A Guide for Parents, 3rd Edition (2003) Sara Graefe

Challenge of Fetal Alcohol Syndrome; Overcoming Secondary Disabilities (1997) Ann Streissguth and Jonathan Kanter.

Fetal Alcohol Syndrome: A Guide for Families and Communities (1997) Ann Streissguth

Fantastic Antone Succeeds! (1993) Judith Kleinfeld and Siobhan Wescott

PRENATAL DRUG EXPOSURE

Working with Children and Families Affected by Substance Abuse (1996) Kathleen Pullan Watkins and Lucius Durant.

Living with Prenatal Drug Exposure: A Guide for Parents (2003) Lissa Cowan and Jennifer Lee (forthcoming)

ATTENTION DEFICIT HYPERACTIVITY DISORDER

Beyond Ritalin (1997) Stephen Garber, Marianne Daniels Garber, Robyn Spizman

Beyond ADD (1996) Thom Hartmann

Teenagers with ADD, a Parents' Guide (1995) Chris A. Zeigler Dendy

CONDUCT DISORDER

Raising Children Who Refuse to Be Raised (2000) Dave Ziegler

Treating the Unmanageable Adolescent: a Guide to Oppositional Defiant and Conduct Disorders (1997) Neil Bernstein

ABUSE & NEGLECT

Parenting Traumatized Children: a Survival Guide for Parents and Professionals (1997) Dee Paddock (audio)

Emotional Child Abuse (1996) Joel Covitz

When Children Abuse (1996) Carolyn Cunningham and Kee MacFarlane.

Adopting or Fostering a Sexually Abused Child (1999) C. MacAskill

The Courage to Heal (1988) Ellen Bass and Laura Davis

MENTAL HEALTH

Healing Power of the Family: An Illustrated Overview of Life with the Disturbed Foster or Adopted Child (1997) Richard J. Delaney

A Parent's Guide to Childhood and Adolescent Depression (1994) Patricia Gottlieb Shapiro

INSTITUTIONS & CHILDREN

Help for the Hopeless Child, A Guide for Families with Special Discussion for Assessing and Treating the Post Institutionalized Child (1998) Dr. Ronald S. Federici

Adopting the Hurt Child (1995) Gregory Keck and Regina Kupekcy

TRANSITION TO ADULTHOOD

PLAN: How it Works (1998) Al Etmanski

Fantastic Atone Grows Up (2000) Judith Kleinfeld, Barbara Morse and Siobhan Wescott

Web Resources

BC Ministry for Children and Families Development: www.mcf.gov.bc.ca/adoption
Adoption Council of Canada: www.adoption.ca
Canada Adopts: www.canadaadopts.com
Canadopt: www.canadopt.ca
North American Council on Adoptable Children: www.nacac.org

BC Parent Advisory Committee: www.bccpac.bc.ca
Parenting Special Needs: www.familyfocus.com

Child abuse Prevention Network: http://child_abuse.com

Children and Adults with Attention Deficit Disorder Canada (CHADD)
www.chaddcanada.org

FAS Bookshelf Inc.: www.fasbookshelf.com
Canadian Centre on Substance Abuse: www.ccsa.ca
Asante Centre for Fetal Alcohol Syndrome: www.asantecentre.org

LDA Canada: www.ldac_taac.ca
LDA Vancouver: www.ldav.ca

Health Canada: www.hc-sc.gc.ca
Mental Health Net: www.mentalhelp.net

Neonatal Abstinence: http://neonatal.peds.washington.edu/NICU_WEB/nas.htm
High Risk: http://www.lpch.org/HealthLibrary/ChildrensHealthAZ/hrnewborn/nas.htm

Learning Disabilities Association of Canada: www.ldac-taac.ca

Planned Lifetime Advocacy Network: www.plan.ca

Organizations

The Society of Special Needs Adoptive Parents (SNAP)
1-800-663-7627, www.snap.bc.ca

Adoption Council of Canada
613-235-0344, www.adoption.ca

North American Council on Adoptable Children
651-644-3036, www.nacac.org

acknowledgements

A book series of this scope would not have been possible without the help of various individuals and organizations. The editor would like to acknowledge the following:

Brad Watson and the Society of Special Needs Adoptive Parents (SNAP), for kick-starting this project, and Susan Lees and the Adoption Support Program at the Queen Alexandra Centre for Children's Health, for support and financial assistance;

The British Columbia Ministry for Children and Family Development, for funding support for the production of this series;

Jennifer Lee of Ben Simon Press, for her editorial, design, and project management; Lissa Cowan, also of Ben Simon Press, for project direction;

Elyssa Schmid of Radiant Design, for her cover designs and layout direction;

Verna Booth in the SNAP library, for research assistance and long hours spent compiling the resource lists;

Emilie Cameron and Neil Carey, for additional research support;

Dolores Talavera, Maria Mercado-Koyanagi, Neil Carey and SNAP office volunteers, for their help securing reprint permission for various articles;

Susan Cowan, Coordinator of Volunteer Programs at SNAP, for liaising with contributing adoptive parents;

The many adoptive families and professionals who were willing to contribute their expertise and personal stories for this collection;

And the many authors and publishers who allowed us to use their material in this series. Specific copyright acknowledgement follows each individual article.

contributors

Verna Booth is SNAP's librarian, and has been with the organization since its very beginning. She has a background as a psychiatric nurse, and is a long-time advocate for individuals with learning disabilities and other special needs.

Francine Bruce is a BC adoptive mom who served for several years as a SNAP Resource Parent.

Stacey Burnard is a district Special Education Resource teacher in Port Alberni, BC. She is responsible for the programming, assessment and mental health counselling for middle school children.

Patty Burk is a SNAP Resource Parent and facilitator for SNAP's support group in Nanaimo. She and her husband Tom parent three children, one of whom has multiple mental illness diagnoses.

Vickie Cammack is Executive Director of Planned Lifetime Advocacy Network Institute for Citizenship and Disability in Burnaby, BC.

Julianne Conry, Ph.D. is a long-time SNAP Board member and specialist in child behaviour and development in the Department of Educational Psychology and Special Education at the University of British Columbia. She recently co-authored, with Dr. Diane Fast, the book *Fetal Alcohol Syndrome and the Criminal Justice System*.

Lissa Cowan is the Editorial Director of Ben Simon Press, Managing Editor of *Family Groundwork Magazine*, and Communications Consultant for SNAP Promotions. She lives on Vancouver Island and works part-time as a writer and translator. She is currently working on a French to English poetry translation.

Isaac de Bree was an adopted person affected by FAS. He died tragically in a suicide-related accident in May 2002, but his spirit remains alive to the many people who knew and cared about him.

Ro de Bree is a long-time SNAP resource parent living in Duncan, BC. She has written and published extensively about her experiences parenting adoptive children with Fetal Alcohol Syndrome.

Tanis Doe is an educator and sexual abuse consultant. She is a non-hearing, single adoptive parent, and long-time SNAP member.

Linda Duck is a Canadian Certified Family Educator with Family Services Canada and a Certified Special Needs Teaching Assistant with the Richmond School Board. She has six children, two of whom have special needs.

Al Etmanski is the Executive Director of PLAN – Planned Lifetime Advocacy Network in Burnaby, BC.

Lorelei Faulkner is currently the Clinical Nurse and Coordinator for the ADHD Assessment Clinic at Children's and Women's Health Centre in Vancouver. Lorelei also sits on the professional advisory board for CHADD Vancouver.

Dr. Ronald S. Federici is a Developmental Neuropsychologist and is President/ CEO for Care for Children International, Inc. He is also Clinical Director of Neuropsychological and Family Therapy Associates, P.C.

Carol Fyfe-Wilson is a SNAP Resource Parent who, with her husband, adopted three children from Haiti, having already raised 5 children. She has had a diverse career in the public and private sectors, most recently as Special Education Aide and peer counsellor.

Sara Graefe served the adoption community for five years in her role as SNAP's former Publications Coordinator. She is the editor and principal writer of SNAP's best-selling book, *Parenting Children Affected by Fetal Alcohol Syndrome: A Guide for Daily Living.* She currently works in Vancouver as a freelance writer, and in the story department of *Edgemont,* CBC's television series for youth.

Lisa Marie Gruger is a couple and family therapist based in Langley, BC, where she works with those touched by adoption. Her extensive experience encompasses special needs adoption, behaviour disorders, psychiatric disorders, learning disabilities, as well as attachment and bonding. She is on the Board of Directors for the Greater Vancouver Fetal Alcohol Society (The Asante Centre). She is also a former coordinator for SNAP's Volunteer and Education Programs.

Jane Holland is an advocate for adult services for people with special needs. She is the former Director of the Family Support Institute, Vancouver.

Dr. Frank Kunstal is therapist working with special needs children in Fort Collins, Colorado.

Jennifer Lee is the General Manager of Ben Simon Press, Editor in Chief of *Family Groundwork Magazine* and Communications Consultant for SNAP Promotions. She is currently working on her second novel and an online arts magazine for youth.

Susan MacRae is originally from Edmonton, Alberta. She has a BFA in Creative Writing from the University of British Columbia and is presently working on her Master's degree in English/Creative Writing at City College in Harlem, USA. She has been a volunteer writer for SNAP since 1997.

Donna McCreesh is a SNAP Resource Parent living in Parksville, BC. She is a retired nurse with experience with Autism Spectrum Disorder and ADHD.

Joan McNamara is an adoption specialist with a placement agency, a parent by birth and adoption, and a renowned author in the field.

Dr. Marlene Moretti is a registered psychologist and professor in the Department of Psychology at Simon Fraser University. Her clinical work and research focus on children, adolescents and the role of family attachment in promoting healthy adolescent attachment. Dr. Moretti's applied work focuses on program development and evaluation within the area of adolescent mental health services.

Beryl Trimble is a SNAP Resource Parent and Coordinator of Maple Ridge FAS/ADD Resource Centre, Maple Ridge, BC.

Karen Van Rheenen is a social worker in British Columbia.

also available from snap & ben simon press

Adoption Piece by Piece (3 volumes):
    Lifelong Issues
    Special Needs
    A Toolkit for Parents
Edited by Sara Graefe
This series represents a comprehensive collection of articles from experienced parents and professionals on a variety of topics related to adoption.

Living with Prenatal Drug Exposure: A Guide for Parents
By Lissa Cowan and Jennifer Lee
This comprehensive book for parents and professionals introduces caregivers to the challenges of caring for a child prenatally exposed to drugs.

Living with FASD: A Guide for Parents, 3rd Edition
By Sara Graefe
This updated 3rd edition includes diagnostic criteria, special considerations for infants and adolescents, and an expanded resource list.

Adoptive Families are Families for Keeps
Text by Lissa Cowan, illustrations by Stephanie Hill
This colouring book will provide social workers, foster parents, caregivers and educators with dynamic and instructive ways to introduce and discuss a wide range of adoption issues with young children.

To order any of these titles, please visit our website at www.snap.bc.ca.